MW00744331

THINK PROPERTY

and

GROW RICH

LIFESUCCESS PUBLISHING, LLC
8900 E Pinnacle Peak Road, Suite D240
Scottsdale, AZ 85255
Telephone: 800.473.7134
Fax: 480.661.1014
E-mail: admin@lifesuccesspublishing.com

ISBN: (hardcover): 978-1-59930-167-9
ISBN: (e-book): 978-1-59930-267-6

Cover : Fiona Dempsey & LifeSuccess Publishing
Layout: Fiona Dempsey & LifeSuccess Publishing

COMPANIES, ORGANIZATIONS,
INSTITUTIONS, AND INDUSTRY PUBLICATIONS:
Quantity discounts are available on bulk purchases of this book for reselling,
educational purposes, subscription incentives, gifts,
sponsorship, or fundraising. Special books or book excerpts can also
be created to fit specific needs such as private labeling with your logo
on the cover and a message from a VIP printed inside.
FOR MORE INFORMATION PLEASE CONTACT OUR
SPECIAL SALES DEPARTMENT AT
LIFESUCCESS PUBLISHING.

PRINTED IN CANADA

THINK PROPERTY

and

GROW RICH

*Master buying Australian investment
properties in changing times
like the experts do*

MELAINIE WHITE

TESTIMONIALS

*Melainie's wealth of experience shines through in this practical
"out of the square" book on increasing net wealth through property
investment. Her underlying theme is to set your investing goals and
then plan to achieve them. Each chapter is followed with a list of key
points and a page where the reader completes his/her action plan and
notes. Melainie says, 'There is nothing complicated about investing in
property – anyone can do it.' With the help of her book, she is right.*

Tony Compton

Author of ***Rental Property and Taxation***

Brisbane, QLD, Australia

*Melainie, thank you so much for demystifying the subject of property
investment. Your excellent book is easy to read and understand while
being absolutely packed with quality information and insight. I
loved how your book gives both the strategic mindset as well as the
tactical approach for success in property investing. We are so grateful
that we have been able to draw on your expertise as a guide through
the maze of buying property. Think Property and Grow Rich is an
absolute 'must read' for anyone looking at getting into the Australian
property market. Apart from that, it is full of wisdom on how to
grow a business and achieve personal goals.
Put it at the top of your list.*

Irena Yashin-Shaw, PhD

Professional Speaker, Author

Director of Speaking Edge and Innovation Edge

Brisbane, QLD, Australia

Knowledge is priceless, so is this book! Thank you, Melainie.

Dean Vegas

World-Renowned Entertainer, Property Investor

Gold Coast, QLD, Australia

*Congratulations, Melainie, for putting together a book
that delivers a wealth of information on how to develop
your property portfolio. You have kept things simple and easily
understood. Well done.*

John Salton

Author of *Get the Renovation You Really Want*

Melbourne, VIC, Australia

*Melainie has completely demystified the property-investment
market. Her book has given us the simplest path to follow to
make property part of our future.
A must read for all investors.*

Paul & Shelley Fox

Authors, *Diamonds Demystified*

Booval Hourglass Jewellers

Ipswich, QLD, Australia

TESTIMONIALS

This book is packed full of powerful, practical, and easy to understand advice and therefore easy to implement. Follow this advice and you will wish you had read this book a lot earlier.

Gerry Robert

Bestselling Author of *The Millionaire Mindset*

Toronto, Canada

Think Property and Grow Rich is a book that is an invaluable tool for the person wanting to increase wealth and to produce positive financial outcomes in following the right steps in purchasing property. There are also tips for renovating to increase property values, a must read.

Mark Turra

Turra Builders/Carpenters

Cobram, VIC, Australia

DEDICATION

To Gary: your support, encouragement, and belief have helped me make this book a reality. Thank you for your understanding throughout this process. I will always be grateful for all that you have done and all that you do for me. A dream with a plan is a goal.

And to all those people who know that there is more to life than what society teaches, and who want to make a difference in their own and others' lives. Dream and plan your future today.

DISCLAIMER

Great care has been taken in the writing and researching of this book. This work represents the personal experience and opinions of the author and, as such, should not be taken as investment advice. The reader assumes all risk for any actions taken based upon the content or comments in this work. The author bears no responsibility for omissions or errors; the text is intended as general commentary only, and is not to be considered comprehensive in any way. It is advised that each person seek competent and current advice from qualified professionals before investing.

CONTENTS

FOREWORD

For more than forty years, I've helped people understand the principles of increasing their personal wealth. In that time, I can honestly say that it is not about the opportunity you choose to pursue, but it is about overcoming your own fears and self-limiting beliefs. It is not until you choose to set aside those fears and insecurities that you experience the unlimited abundance that exists all around you.

Melainie White understands these principles and has used them to grow her property business. She knows what it's like to let fear get the best of you, and also how to overcome resistance to change. Her book, *Think Property and Grow Rich,* explains how you can educate yourself about buying property to create the wealth you desire.

Real estate has long been one of the greatest investments you can hold, and many of the world's wealthiest people have become so due to their real estate holdings. While you may perceive the property market to be intimidating, it doesn't have to be. Melainie can guide you through every step of the process, whether you are buying your first home or your tenth investment property.

The real change starts within, as you visualize what your life can be like when you no longer worry about money. I often speak of creating multiple streams of income, and that's exactly what property investment is – many streams of income flowing to you without your direct involvement. It all begins with a decision to set aside those fears and pursue your dreams. Make that decision right now and step into a life of financial freedom.

Bob Proctor, featured in *The Secret*
Author of *You Were Born Rich*

ACKNOWLEDGEMENTS

To all the wonderful people who have supported my dream of putting this book together, THANK YOU!

Dee, thank you for your friendship and for all our chats. You have an incredible wealth of knowledge. Here's cheers to property investment!

To Gary, for all of your help. Thank you for sharing your unbiased opinions and input.

To my Mum and Dad (Barbara and Alistair White), thank you for being my parents and for giving me love and my foundations in life. Our dairy-farming life was perfect.

To Kevin and Beryl Rigby, thank you for caring about everything I am and do. Kevin, a special thanks for your input.

My dear friend Wendy Carrafa, the love and gratitude I feel for you is more than words can say. Thank you for your inspiration, guidance, support, love, and patience with all my questions.

Thank you to all my clients over the years who have become, in a sense, teachers.

Thank you, Bob Proctor, for believing in my book and writing the foreword. Your teachings have always inspired me.

Thank you to the LifeSuccess Publishing Team, especially Paul Fox – your support is appreciated.

Finally, thank you to all that invest in this book. I trust *Think Property and Grow Rich* helps you in your journey for financial freedom.

CHAPTER

1

MY FUTURE: WHAT DO I REALLY WANT IN MY LIFE?

CHAPTER 1

MY FUTURE:
WHAT DO I REALLY WANT IN MY LIFE?

Effort and courage are not enough without
purpose and direction.
– John F. Kennedy (1917 – 63),
President of the United States of America (1960 – 63)

D o you think about the future? How will you live, what will you accomplish, and where will you be years from now? We all know people who have big dreams and ideas that we consider a little farfetched, but how often have you attended a reunion, or run into an old school friend, to learn that they actually accomplished those dreams? Have you ever had a moment to yourself on a New Year's Eve and felt a little disappointed to think about the previous year, and to know your life hasn't progressed one bit? You are no closer to living a worry-free existence, having that great vacation home, or planning a wonderful retirement. You feel stuck in the money rut of life, just spinning your tyres and getting covered with mud! Many people live in a constant state of stress over money: how do we get more, keep more, and make sure it won't run out?

NOTE: *While every effort has been made to ensure that all wording in this book is presented in language that is easy to understand, I have provided, at the rear of this book, a full glossary of real estate terms to assist in your understanding.*

WE LIVE WITHIN a range in life, accepting what we think we can achieve, and our vision tends to narrow with time, until we find ourselves locked in a cage of our own making. I've done this, and maybe you have too. I once lived just like everyone else. I made certain assumptions about myself and what I could accomplish. Unfortunately, those assumptions had little to do with the true reality or my potential. I was able to break away from those false expectations, and I can help you do the same.

First, I will tell you that there is no such thing as a dream too big. Anything is possible, and living a carefree life of financial freedom requires just one thing – money. 'Oh, that's all!' I can hear you saying to yourself. Yes, that is all, and the best way I know to earn great returns while creating substantial cash flow is through property investment. While there are numerous investment options in the marketplace, property investment allows you to meet dual goals: money to live on later (capital appreciation), and money to live on now (cash flow). It is one of the few investments that literally allow you to have your cake and eat it too!

It amazes me how often I talk about creating wealth from property investment, only to meet with incredible resistance from the very people who could most benefit. They repeatedly say that property investment is too complex, or not for them, and turn their backs on the opportunity to change their lives. Why? Literally millions of people, in every part of the country, and throughout the world, invest in property. Does this mean that they are somehow smarter than average? I'm here to tell you that they are not. They were just willing to learn something new.

You and I have the ability to control our lives. Fate or unwillingness to try is often used as an excuse for not achieving and realising our true potential. It is so much easier just to say, 'It wasn't meant to be' or 'I could never do that'. It is also true that life can throw numerous obstacles in our path, but many of these we cultivate and bring upon ourselves. Just as we can create disappointments, difficulties, and challenges, we can also create happiness, prosperity, and good fortune. The choice is ours.

Whatever your present lifestyle, it can be changed beyond recognition within two years by applying the principles in this book. Your future days and years are based upon your thoughts, words, deeds, and actions of today, and you have already taken the first step.

Before any of us can bring about what we believe to be our perfect lifestyle, we need to know exactly what it is that we really want. We wouldn't go to a railway station and ask for a ticket without knowing our destination. It is the same with achieving our financial dreams. We must know precisely where we want to end up. Is it a nice little house, or a mansion by the sea? What income do we want? How much money in the bank? With whom do we want to share our lives? And what about being happy? Money isn't much good if we are depressed and miserable.

You have to sit down and really think what it is that you want – in detail. This may take some time, or you may already know what you want to achieve. After you have the idea in mind, take a few minutes and write it out on a piece of paper or in a notebook. This may seem like a difficult task, but I can assure you that once you start writing, your thoughts and ideas will flow easily and naturally, and you will find that what you truly desire in life will illuminate itself to you. This process is one of the most productive ways to spend a day.

You most likely already do this in your life today without realising that you are doing so. If you run a business or even work for someone, do you regularly write in your diary a plan for your day ahead, or for what you want and need to achieve that day or week? Writing down what you want in your life is no different than planning out your working day or writing a shopping list for your life – it is just on larger scale. How often do you really think about your life and where it's going in any sort of meaningful way? Most of us merely wander through our daily lives, pushing aside the past, dealing with the present, and refusing to think about the future. By doing this one exercise, it can bring your life into perspective and give you control over circumstance.

MY FUTURE: WHAT DO I REALLY WANT IN MY LIFE?

It is important to note that whatever is on your list must be your own thoughts and ambitions and not those of a relation, spouse, or teacher. It cannot be something that you have been taught or brainwashed with since childhood. It is important to keep secret any wishes that you feel those close to you may laugh at or criticise. The negative comments of other people can prevent us from reaching fulfilment by deflecting us away from the things that we really want and need.

After you have completed your list, you need to divide your wishes into three sections:

1.   What you want right now.

2.   Your medium-term wishes and ambitions.

3.   Your long-term perfect life.

UNDER SECTION ONE, list things you want right now – such as paying off your credit cards, spending more time with the children, losing a few pounds or kilos, being more understanding of your spouse, getting a new job, and so on.

Section two may possibly include a new car, a higher income, money in a savings account, a holiday abroad, or new furniture.

Section three is what you see as your perfect life. Perhaps this includes a house overlooking the sea, a luxury car in the driveway, a high income, money in the bank, a stress-free, happy life with your partner and children, or lots of time to travel the world and help others. Let your imagination run wild as you envision whatever it is that you really want.

The next thing to do is to look at your list again and become more specific with everything. What exactly is it that you want? A 'higher income' isn't being specific, nor is 'money in the bank'. How much income do you want? $1000, $5000, $10,000, $50,000, $100,000? Or more? How much money do you want in the bank? What sort of car do you want in your driveway – the model, make, and colour?

All ambitions, targets, and objectives should be time-related, but be aware that if you say something like, 'I want a million dollars by next month', you probably won't believe this to be possible. Neither will your subconscious, especially if you have been moaning about not having any money for years and years. But, in saying this, there is no reason why you can't become a millionaire, if that is truly what you want. Just give it a longer time frame.

As an example, if one of your goals is a 'higher income', this could be changed to something like, 'I want an income of $10,000 per month by December 31 of this year', or something similar. By just participating in this exercise, your goals become clearer and your mind will be able to focus on what you want. This allows you to recognise solutions and opportunities when they come along. Truly, the solutions already exist to meet all of your dreams, but since you haven't been focused on them, you have been unable to seize the opportunities that will bring you what you want.

It is very much like when you buy a new car. Let's say you buy a red car because you feel it's unique and will stand out. The minute you drive the car from the dealership, you notice every single red car – and marvel at how many there are! The only difference is that you are aware of them now, where before they just passed through your peripheral vision without you even noticing.

This is an important point, because if you have been unfamiliar with property investments, you may feel that you won't be able to get the information you need to be successful. However, once you decide to focus on properties, you will be overwhelmed by the information and people that come forward to help you. Actually, they were always there and are there right now; you just didn't notice them because you weren't interested.

Life is really quite simple, but most of us look upon it as being something of an uphill struggle – a battle to be fought against a flow of continuous challenges, difficulties, and worries. The fact is, however, that we are creative beings, and as such can bring about a life full of happiness, wealth, and health.

Our thoughts, words, deeds, and actions of yesterday have created the life that we are living today. This may sound like psycho-babble, but, nevertheless, I believe this to be true. If I am right, it stands to reason that the things we think, say, and do today will, therefore, determine our future.

All that we are is the result of what we have thought.
– Buddha (563 BC – 483 BC)

HERE'S A VERY simple example. I have a friend who for years has disliked the Christmas season. If you were to ask him if he was looking forward to Christmas, he would say something like, 'Not really. I am waiting to see what will go wrong this year'. He's never disappointed! Every year something happens to ruin his Christmas, just as he visualises and expects. His wife takes ill, his water pipes burst, or his car breaks down. Coincidence? I don't think so.

If we can accept that we can create our futures, this should make us more careful about our thoughts and actions. If we keep saying that we haven't got any money, we won't have any. If we cannot visualize our circumstances ever changing, they won't. If we believe it is a waste of time trying something new, it is. If we see challenges ahead, there will be challenges. But, if we can look at life differently, we can start a flow of good and can attract the things that we really want.

I just had you make out a list of the things that you want now, your medium-term goals, and also your long-term perfect life. If you look at this as being fanciful, wishful thinking, and a waste of time, it will be all those things. Conversely, you may believe that perhaps there is something in all of this and that you really can have the things you want. If this is the case, I urge you to alter your way of thinking and your life can be transformed. In order for this to happen, you have to believe that your goals and dreams can materialise.

Start by reading your list as many times a day as possible, especially first thing in the morning and last thing before you go to sleep. Cut out pictures of the things you want from magazines and catalogues, and stick them into a scrapbook or on a wall chart. Look at them every day to reinforce in your mind that these are the things that you want.

It is strange, but when we start thinking about something, associated things keep coming to our attention – like the red cars. The mind has a filtering system. If we were to take in and be conscious of every little thing we saw during the day, it would all be too much. The mind lets us see what it thinks is important. It picks out useful information relevant to our lives and to what we have been thinking and talking about. When we had the discussion about seeing red cars instead of filtering them out, as your mind had previously done, they were brought to your attention instead. This can also happen with things that we want. Whereas previously opportunities and relevant information were overlooked, the mind now brings these to your conscious attention.

Your words must match this new awareness and reinforce what you want. It is no good looking at your scrapbook and seeing lots of money, and then to keep saying how poor you are. Your words have to alter so that they do not conflict with what you want. You must start to believe that you already have the things that you desire. One of the best ways to do this is by visualization.

The thing always happens that you really believe in; and the belief in a thing makes it happen.
– Frank Lloyd Wright (1869 – 1959), American Architect

THE SUBCONSCIOUS WORKS in pictures, not abstract ideas. Therefore, if you create the right pictures in your mind, your mind will believe them to be true and will help bring them into your life. There are many visualization techniques, but they all have the same objective, which is to create a picture of some desired object or event and to bring this into reality.

The easiest way to visualise is to sit quietly with your eyes closed. Breathe deeply and focus on creating a detailed picture in your mind of what your life will be like when you attain your desires. Picture how it will look, feel, sound, and taste. This creates a vivid image that your mind becomes emotionally involved with. By bringing these details into the conscious mind, it will then look for and associate things that belong in that image. You will become aware of opportunities and people who can help you get what you want because you have trained your mind to be aware of how you want your life to be.

That is all there is to it! If this is something you have never heard about before, it may all sound silly and unbelievable, but if you have carried out this exercise, you have taken the first steps to creating something in your life by using your mind alone. Whatever it is that you want will, at the right time, come about. You may have to repeat the same exercise several times for the same dream, but it will arrive in its own way.

It is not up to you as to how this will come about, and you shouldn't try to imagine how it may happen. It is like posting a letter. After you have popped it into the box, you don't then start thinking about how the letter will arrive, how the sorting office will put it in a sack for delivery, how the letter will travel first by train and then by van, and so on. You just post your letter and forget about it. It is same with using the mind. You release the image knowing that what you give out, you will receive.

It does take a bit of effort and self-discipline for us to control our words and thoughts, as it is so easy to agree and be swept along by others when they are moaning about their life and things in general. A lot of people delight in dwelling on everything that is wrong with the world. They are rarely ever happy, healthy, and successful people.

There is, in effect, no reality in life. There is just our perception of how things are. The old saying about the half-empty or half-full glass is perfectly true. Everything is how we perceive it to be, and the next person may perceive it to be completely the opposite.

Critics often speak of 'the rich' with none-too-subtle disdain, as if those at the top of the income ladder all are crooks, or as if becoming rich is difficult and means that others must become poorer. This is not true. There is an unlimited supply of wealth. You can compare it to air. If we were all to stand in a circle and breathe in, and then hold our breath, would that mean there was less oxygen for everyone else? Of course not. There is an abundance for everyone, and more than enough to go around. This fact suggests that becoming rich is largely a matter of choice. Contrary to the beliefs of some, the pursuit of wealth is not bad, nor does it indicate a lack of caring toward your fellow man – indeed, it is quite the opposite. Imagine how many people you could help if you were a multimillionaire. Think of how it could change the lives of so many just because you chose wealth.

THE INVESTOR IN US ALL

MOST PEOPLE KNOW they should invest, just as most people know they should watch their diet and exercise. Nonetheless, millions of people – easily 80 to 85 per cent of Australians – don't invest at all. What I mean by this is that these people are not active investors.

An active investor is someone who actually lives off their investments, as opposed to wages from a job. The goal of the investor is to receive a stream of cash flow every month, which removes the necessity of a job.

It's similar to the difference between amateur and professional golfers: Amateurs may be very good players, but can they live off their golf game? A professional can withstand the heat of competition, and has the mental toughness and the physical skills to create a stream of income from playing the game.

Stand for something or fall for anything.
– John Mellencamp, American Singer and Songwriter

DO YOU KNOW that if you went to a school reunion of 100 people, only 5 of you will be financially independent when you all reach retirement? The rest of your former schoolmates will be living on very little, perhaps on even less than the poverty rate. If you and all your schoolmates started out fairly much the same, with similar ideas about life, why is it that only 5 per cent become financially independent, while the rest are average?

If you do what the majority of people do, you will only ever be average. Stand up and be different, and find out what the other 5 per cent are doing. You make the choice. I am sure that if you are reading this book and seeking the answers to create your financial independence, you will find them, but first you must make the decision to go after your dream.

WHY PEOPLE DON'T INVEST

I found every single successful person I've ever spoken to had a turning point. The turning point was when they made a clear, specific, unequivocal decision that they were not going to live like this anymore; they were going to achieve success. Some people make that decision at fifteen and some people make it at fifty, and most people never make it at all.
– Brian Tracy, American Business Philosopher

WHEN I WAS young, I knew there had to be more to life than growing up, getting an education, working until retirement, and then spending my retirement years like my grandparents on a pension until the day I died. I knew that I did not want to have this type of life. I wanted to be able to make my own choices, and this meant I needed money to create my freedom of choice. I really didn't have any idea how or what to do to change my life's path, but I had a burning desire to do so.

I started reading books like *Rich Dad, Poor Dad* by Robert Kiyosaki and *Money* by Paul Clitheroe. I also read books on goals and the power of the mind, like Bob Proctor's *You Were Born Rich* and Napoleon Hill's *Think and Grow Rich.* I also focused upon other helpful books that contained the tools to help me understand the personalities of others and develop my communication skills. Combining my new understanding of myself and what I wanted helped me to move forward in changing my life. I think the number one most important thing you can do for yourself is deciding what you want.

What do you want? I ask this question of people I meet, and I get answers like, "I want to be happy and have enough money in my life." This sounds fantastic, but what is happy? And how much money is enough? Will buying yourself a new house to live in, or getting a new car every two years, be what you need to make yourself happy? Perhaps your idea of happiness is to get married and have children. And what about money? Is having $500,000 or $1,000,000 enough for you to live on during your retirement? I implore you seriously think about what you want and dwell on it in more than a passing fashion. This is really the key to beginning your journey, and it can't be taken lightly.

I think some of the fallacies that people have about their financial future are the following:

1. They think the government will take care of their retirement.

2. They live in the now with no thought to the future.

3. They mistakenly believe they can work forever.

4. They believe expenses will be less as they age and they can live on the money they have put into their home.

Let's look at each one of these issues individually.

THE GOVERNMENT WILL TAKE CARE OF THEM

WHILE THIS IS a nice thought, with baby boomers aging, many pensions and government plans will be cutting services and payments in the future. This isn't unique to Australia. The United States and the United Kingdom will face similar crises. Without an independent source of income, it may become impossible to live on these government plans. In addition, depending on an outside source like the government means that you will be forced to live how and where they tell you to live. You will have to follow their rules for services such as health care, and this dependence removes your choice to receive the best care possible.

THEY LIVE IN THE NOW WITH NO THOUGHT TO THE FUTURE

TIME SLIPS AWAY from us all, but time is also our biggest friend when it comes to investing. This is due to the effect of compounding. Compounding means you make money on the original investment, as well as the earnings, each year. This allows your money to grow exponentially, rather than at a flat rate. By putting off the thought of how to invest or make more money than you are currently earning, you are actually costing yourself money that will never be earned by compounding. This is not to say that it is ever too late to begin. No matter what a person's age, property can provide the necessary cash flow that can make all the difference in lifestyle.

THEY BELIEVE THEY CAN WORK FOREVER

IN REALITY, VERY few people are able to maintain their health into their seventies or eighties, and even if they did, few employers would hire them. Even if you were in perfect health and could work all day into your nineties, would you want that? One of the best things about achieving financial freedom through property investment is that it gives you the power to choose – not only how you live, but where you live and whether you will work full time. Should you be laid up or need some short-term medical care, your properties will still produce a stream of cash to help through those times.

THEY BELIEVE EXPENSES WILL BE LESS AS THEY AGE, AND THEY CAN LIVE ON MONEY THEY HAVE PUT INTO THEIR HOME

WHILE IT'S TRUE that most people become less consumer-minded as they age, that doesn't mean that expenses decrease. They may not go out to the movies each week, but they might have additional medications and doctor visits. One of the biggest mistakes people make is to assume that they can live on a given amount twenty years from now, when they are basing expenses on today's dollars. The price of everything goes up, and over twenty years, prices go up tremendously. No matter what amount you think you can live on, it's always good to have additional income flowing in, just in case you're off by a few thousand – or tens of thousands.

Make a decision to be successful right now. Most people never
decide to be wealthy and that is why they retire poor.
– Brian Tracy, American Business Philosopher

OFTEN, I'LL HEAR someone say they are putting money into their home and that they will live on that when they need to. My only question is, then, where will they live? A place to live is always a cash drain. It does not produce cash flow, and you still must pay for maintenance and insurance. By selling the home, you still must find somewhere else to live at the current market rates, which eat that money up quickly.

Property investment can provide the perfect solution to all of these issues, yet it is one of those things that many people seem to think they shouldn't involve themselves with. This may be because they've simply never done it before, or because they listen to the 'gloom and doom' people who predict that the real estate bubble will burst, or because of tenant horror stories, or because they believe it's going to be too much hard work.

I never allow any difficulties. The great secret of being useful
and successful is to admit no difficulties.
– Sir George Gipps (1791 – 1847),
Former Governor of New South Wales

A FRIEND OF mine just bought and moved in to a new house with his partner, and they are fortunate enough to have been able to buy this house while still owning their own respective homes. However, it now seems that instead of keeping his original house and seeing it as one of the best investment moves he could ever make, he's going to sell it, as he doesn't wasn't the hassle/ heartache/challenges that he believes property management will bring.

My argument is completely the opposite. If that home is worth $200,000, then, theoretically, it will double in value over the next seven to ten years. Can you think of many other investment opportunities that will deliver you $200,000 profit in about seven years? Any suggestions? I don't know of any pension that would do that!

Following are a few quick facts that should convince you that property investing might be the way to go for you:

- Property has historically doubled in value every seven to ten years.

- You don't need to look after the property yourself – simply employ the services of a managing agent.

- After you've bought your first property, you can keep buying more properties as slowly or as quickly as your investments will allow. Simply choose the financing strategy that will work best for your own circumstances.

- There are certain tax benefits you can use by offsetting everyday costs against your property investments. The basic cost of doing business, such as expenses associated with your properties, including property maintenance, legal fees, and any real estate fees and any associated cost, can be offset as a business expense.

- When you remortgage the property you live in, you don't pay any tax on the equity that you take out of it.

- Pensions are, on the whole, not producing the returns we all need to keep us comfortable (or in the lap of luxury), so invest in something that has much better prospects.

PROPERTY ALWAYS HAS been – and always will be – the best, most simple way for anyone to build wealth. If you own your own home, how much has it gone up in value since you bought it? This is your chance to build wealth as a property entrepreneur. It doesn't matter if you have little or no experience. Anyone can be a successful property investor. If you can learn a few simple techniques, you can make good money from it.

Quite simply, property millionaires outnumber those of any other investment class. Those who haven't made their money directly from property generally invest in it indirectly through trusts or investment groups. Remember, there's nothing wrong with seeing what successful people do and applying those principles to your own life.

If the majority of extraordinarily wealthy people have used property profitably, it stands to reason that there's money to be made in this sector. Property investment is not just for the wealthy. It doesn't really take large sums of money to get involved in real estate. This is because banks will lend up to 90 per cent, and sometimes even over 100 per cent against the security of residential property, which means that most people with a steady job and a little capital behind them can afford to buy investment properties.

Banks have always recognised property, and especially residential property, as an excellent security. The reason they'll lend you such a high percentage of the value of your property is that they know that property values have never fallen over the long term.

Another factor contributing to the security of property investment is the high percentage of owner-occupiers, which means people owning or paying off their own homes. Owner-occupiers outweigh investors by a huge amount, which means that residential property is the only investment market not dominated by investors. This effectively gives investors a built-in safety net. Even if all the investors were to leave the market at once, it would not totally collapse since the vast majority of homes are owned by individuals.

The rental income you receive from your investment property allows you to borrow and obtain the benefit of leverage by helping you pay the interest on your mortgage. Over the years, the rental income received from property investments will increase, particularly in times of a slower market and higher inflation.

Residential property has an unequalled track record of producing high and consistent capital growth. If you pay for your purchase using all cash (without getting a loan), the return you get on the property isn't much higher than what you could achieve with other types of investments.

The ability to use leverage with property significantly increases the amount of profit you can make and, importantly, it allows you to purchase a significantly larger investment than you would normally be able to afford.

Property is a great investment because you make all the decisions and have direct control over the returns from your property. If your property is not producing good returns, then you can add value through refurbishment, renovations, additional furniture, or other changes to make the property more desirable to tenants. In other words, you can directly influence your returns by taking an interest in your property, and by understanding and then meeting the needs of prospective tenants. You can't do this with other types of investments.

There are hundreds of ways you can add value to your property that will increase your income and your property's capital value. These include little things like giving it a coat of paint, or removing the old carpet and polishing the floorboards underneath. Or you could do major renovations or development works. Unlike most other investments, when property goes up in value, you don't need to sell in order to capitalise on that increased value. You simply go back to your bank or mortgage broker and get your lender to increase your loan. Even if you bought the worst house at the worst possible time, the chances are good that it would still go up in value over the next few years. History has proven that property is possibly the most forgiving investment asset over time. If you are prepared to hold the property over a number of years, it's almost guaranteed to rise in value. There's really no other asset class quite like property!

There's also nothing complicated about investing in property. You can invest as little or as much as you like. It all depends on how much money you want to make. You might just want to buy the odd property here and there, build up a substantial portfolio, and eventually live in a home in the sun. Within a short while, you'll establish a monthly income that just grows and grows – and you hardly have to do anything to get it. This is income or retirement money that you don't have to depend on anyone else to receive. You make it. It's yours and yours alone. Unlike other asset classes, property value never disappears. It won't go bankrupt or drop to zero, like Enron, HIH, and so many other 'can't lose' share companies that turned into disasters. Property, on the other hand, is one of the oldest investment opportunities there is. Its success has been proven over hundreds – even thousands – of years.

You gain strength, courage and confidence by every experience
in which you really stop to look fear in the face.... You must
do the thing you cannot do.
– Eleanor Roosevelt (1884 – 1962),
First Lady of the United States, (1933 – 45)

DON'T YOU THINK it's time you put aside your excuses and fear and began to create the life of your dreams?

CHAPTER 1
MY FUTURE

1. What do you really want out of life, and how do you think it will happen?

2. Property investing is traditionally one of the most solid and sustainable asset classes in the world.

3. By generating additional income that is not dependent on anyone else, you have the choice of how you will live in the future.

4. Property investing does not require a great deal of cash.

5. Many people mistakenly think that property investing is complicated, but it's not.

6. Property investing has created more millionaires than any other asset class.

7. Embark on the journey to true financial independence, and your wealth begins.

MY ACTION PLAN AND NOTES

_____

_____

_____

_____

_____

_____

_____

_____

_____

_____

_____

CHAPTER

2

MY QUESTION:

WHY INVEST IN

PROPERTY?

MY QUESTION:
WHY INVEST IN PROPERTY?

In the middle of difficulty lies opportunity.
– Albert Einstein (1879 – 1955)

H ave you ever considered what your life would be like if you had enough money to really afford a comfortable lifestyle? Even those who consider themselves comfortable often worry if they will have enough to carry them through times of ill health or old age, or to provide for the family when they are no longer around. What would it be like to have so much coming in that you didn't notice the pinch of inflation or the rising price of fuel?

While it is true that money can't make us happy, having enough does make a huge difference in how we live our lives. I know that money does not change personal happiness, but I know through my own experience that when you don't have enough money, you can be unhappy due to the worry and stress of meeting financial commitments. We need money to be secure and comfortable, and there are a total of three ways to create that security for ourselves – yes, just three:

- Working

- Saving

- Investing

NOTICE I DIDN'T include inherited money or lottery winnings. While it is possible to receive money from these sources, they are not through your own creation, so we'll leave them in a separate category for now.

WORKING

WORKING AS A salary or wage earner creates an income, which is then taxed. This after-tax income is what most of us use to purchase items that involve our daily living. If we plan well enough, we may also save some of the income in retirement plans, such as Superannuation Funds, so that we can maintain our standard of living, or travel. This will allow us to do as we please when we are too old to work and no longer have the ability or desire to work a regular job. In addition, we can purchase life insurance with our earned income to ensure that we and our families can maintain our standard of living in the event of ill health or death. Though working does meet our needs, when we work there is only a limited amount of time for us to earn, and for most people, they must compromise on their wants and dreams in order to live within that finite budget.

Many of us are brought up to get a good education and then secure a job, and then work all our lives for as long as we are able. This is how it has been for many generations before us. But this is no longer the best avenue to achieve your dreams. We have all watched our parents and parents' friends take this exact advice from their parents, most of whom are today relying on the old age pension to live out their so-called twilight years. From what I see, this pension they receive only allows for food and a basic standard of living. I know many from older generations would have loved to have been given advice about planning for their future and investing in property, rather than the advice they received that encouraged them to work until a certain age, and then live the rest of their lives on tight budgets.

Think of it this way: if we continue to follow exactly the path that previous generations followed, we will be living on tight budgets when we retire as well. I know that I have other choices, and I choose to live my twilight years with many options. Therefore, I decided years ago to do it differently – and so can you.

The people who get on in this world are the people who get up and look for the circumstances they want, and, if they can't find them, make them.
– George Bernard Shaw (1856 – 1950),
Irish Dramatist, Essayist, and Critic

SAVING

SAVING ACCUMULATES PORTFOLIO income and can be in the form of interest or dividends. Portfolio income, if used in full, has the tendency to lose its buying power over time, due to the negative effect of inflation. In other words, we can't buy as much today with our dollars as we did yesterday. Inflation will always be a fact of life, which is why when people plan to retire, they must plan to have significantly more income than they do right now, since that money will not go as far. One thing that saving allows us to do is create assets. Assets are investments that produce income (like property), and when managed wisely, can replace the need to earn a living or carry large amounts of insurance.

Few people really understand the power of savings with compounding growth. The way compounding works is that interest earned and added to your initial savings grows at a high rate. For example, if you doubled one dollar each week for nineteen weeks, you would accumulate $262,144. This is the theory of compounding. It is powerful, and much underestimated.

Week 1	Week 2	Week 3	Week 4	Week 5
1	2	4	8	16
Week 6	Week 7	Week 8	Week 9	Week 10
32	64	128	256	512
Week 11	Week 12	Week 13	Week 14	Week 15
1,024	2,048	4,096	8,192	16,384
Week 16	Week 17	Week 18	Week 19	
32,768	65,536	131,072	262,144	

SO HOW DOES compounding relate to property? This is where the real power of property investment works in the compounding of growth. Let me show you with an example:

Roger and Lucy both have $200,000 each to invest in property. Lucy is a higher risk investor, and decides to invest her $200,000 into a property that achieves a 12 per cent growth rate each year. Roger is a more conservative investor, and chooses a lower-risk property with a growth rate of 6 per cent per annum. After twenty years, Lucy's $200,000 invested at 12 per cent is worth $1,722,552, while Roger's $200,000 at 6 per cent is worth $605,120.

Investment Rate P.A.	At 5 Years	At 10 Years	At 15 Years	At 20 Years
Lucy 200,000 12%	314,704	554,616	977,422	1,722,552
Roger 200,000 6%	252,495	337,896	452,181	605,120

OBVIOUSLY, THE TABLE is a simplified example and should only be used as a guide, but it does show the extreme difference that compounding makes.

INVESTING

INVESTING CREATES AN asset that generates passive income, such as rent on a property or profits from a business venture. The great thing about investing, apart from the benefits of saving, is that it allows us to utilise the negative effect of taxation and inflation to our advantage. Investing allows us to use property as in instrument of wealth creation, which allows for exponential growth.

Property – both open land and buildings in the form of houses, units, and offices – offers numerous benefits for investors. Many assets that investors are investing in today are not really tangible items. Shares in companies, membership in closed corporations, and other forms of investment only give the investor a piece of paper to file. Investment in property is different. It is real and tangible. You can locate the address, drive to the location, and walk inside.

This type of tangible investment allows you to use it as security to obtain financing, as the asset is directly linked to the monetary value at which it can be turned into cash at any given time. If you were to try that with shares, you would find that they would only be worth about half their current value if you wanted to secure a loan from a bank. The reason why security is so important is that it makes it possible to leverage your investment, or, in other words, it allows you to borrow further money against the security of your property.

For one property I bought, I borrowed $234,000, and the property cost me $310,000. One year later, the property had grown in value, so the bank increased the loan by another $40,000, which enabled me to buy another property. Then, eighteen months later, it had grown again in value to over $440,000, and the bank lent me an additional $87,000 to buy further properties. Thus you can see the power of leverage.

Your risk tolerance will determine the level of leverage you use. The following example compares a highly leveraged investor to a mid-level leveraged investor:

Adam and Fiona have decided to sell their family home and move into rental accommodations in order to use the equity in their property to accelerate their retirement funds. Both decide to invest in property according to their risk level.

The total they have to work with is $600,000, and they each get to use 50 per cent of these funds. They both decided to purchase properties worth $300,000 each. Adam, having the higher risk tolerance, decided to leverage his $300,000 into four properties, while Fiona, who is more conservative, used her $300,000 to purchase two properties. Working on the formula that properties double in value approximately every ten years, let's say that they have a growth appreciation rate of 8 per cent per annum. Fiona put down 50 per cent ($150,000) on each property and borrowed the other 50 per cent interest only from the bank. Adam put down 25 per cent ($75,000) on each property and borrowed the additional 75 per cent interest only from the bank. Note that this example does not take into account any fees associated with the purchases.

FIONA'S PORTFOLIO

Year	Rate PA	Two Properties at $300,000 each	Total Increase PA
Start	8%	600,000.00	Nil
1	8%	648,000.00	48,000.00
2	8%	699,840.00	51,840.00
3	8%	755,827.20	55,987.20
4	8%	816,293.38	60,466.18
5	8%	881,596.85	65,303.47
6	8%	952,124.59	70,527.75
7	8%	1,028,294.56	76,169.97
8	8%	1,110,558.13	82,263.56
9	8%	1,199,402.78	88,844.65

Year	Rate PA	Two Properties at $300,000 each	Total Increase PA
10	8%	1,295,355.00	95,952.22
Value			
Less Initial Cost		600,000.00	
Total Capital Gain		$695,355.00	

ADAM'S PORTFOLIO

Year	Rate PA	Four Properties at $300,000 each	Total Increase PA
Start	8%	1,200,000.00	Nil
1	8%	1,296,000.00	96,000.00
2	8%	1,399,680.00	103,680.00
3	8%	1,511,654.40	111,974.40
4	8%	1,632,586.75	120,932.35
5	8%	1,763,193.69	130,606.94
6	8%	1,904,249.19	141,055.50
7	8%	2,056,589.12	152,339.94
8	8%	2,221,116.25	164,527.13
9	8%	2,398,805.55	177,689.30
10	8%	2,590,710.00	191,904.44
Value			
Less Initial Cost		1,200,000.00	
Total Capital Gain		$1,390,710.00	

WITH THIS EXAMPLE, you can see that the gain in appreciation of the properties allows Adam to have a much higher leverage on his initial investment. However, Fiona's investment also more than doubled, which is an excellent return. It is important to invest in the way that you feel most comfortable, and regardless of whether you are conservative or aggressive in mindset, property investment will still make you quite wealthy.

Leverage is a term used to explain the increased benefit that an investor can expect from an asset if someone, such as a bank, finances part of the asset. The interest portion of the investment can be used as an expense to be deducted from taxable income in order to enhance profitability. Security value also contributes positively, due to the fact that an investor can cash in on his investment more easily since it is possible for a buyer to obtain financing more easily on property when compared with other forms of investments. Property investment also utilises the forces of appreciation, as well as depreciation, to the benefit of the investor. Inflation ensures that the replacement value of property continues to rise. This produces ongoing increases in valuations and investment returns over time.

Over the years, rental income from property has proven to be one of the best forms of passive income. In the initial stages of property investment, and depending on the extent of leverage the investor has used, rental income is mainly used to service the loan on the property. This is one of the areas where inflation is beneficial. As the property rent increases over time, the debt service often remains steady or (if an adjustable rate) increases at a lower rate than rents.

SHOW ME THE MONEY!

WHILE MANY OF you may be thinking that this is too good to be true, let me show you a quick illustration of how single-home property investment works.

Carolyn and Grantley are new investors and currently own their own home, which is valued at $300,000. They owe $160,000 on the loan. They increase their mortgage by an additional $100,000, in the form of a line of credit interest only mortgage. They use this line of credit (LOC) to purchase two rental properties valued at $230,000 each. Each home makes barely enough rent ($250/week) to cover the mortgage payments.

Carolyn & Grantley's home	$300,000	debt $260,000	
Property #1	$230,000	debt $180,000	Cash Flow ($250/wk)
Property #2	$230,000	debt $180,000	Cash Flow ($250/wk)
Total	**$560,000**	**debt $360,000**	**Cash Flow ($500/wk)**

AT THIS STAGE, Carolyn and Grantley are able to deduct the interest from the mortgages on their rental properties, as well as associated expenses, such as property maintenance, insurance, real estate management fees, and building depreciation. This offsets against their income, thus reducing their tax paid throughout the year, or allowing a greater tax refund at the end of year. However, over the next few years, rents climb steadily as the value of the properties also rises. During this same time, their loan amount has remained steady. After ten years, they are now gaining substantial positive cash flow through rent from the properties each month, which are valued at roughly double what they were ten years earlier.

This means that with only two rental properties, Carolyn and Grantley have nearly reached millionaire status with a net gain in property value of $860,000! They also have excess cash flow above debt service on the rentals of $480 per week, or $24,960 per year.

The power of property to create wealth can be just that simple – but don't think you have to wait ten years. You can buy many more than two properties with the cash flow and equity in your homes as time progresses, and benefit exponentially from the power of leverage.

THE GREATEST ADVANTAGES OF PROPERTY INVESTMENT

NOW THAT WE have talked a bit about the numbers involved and money to be made, I want to discuss some of the great advantages that property investment has over some other types of investments.

IT'S INSURABLE

FOR THOSE OF you who typically invest in shares, you understand the challenging concept of insuring against potential losses shares can have that proves very difficult, as many insurance companies view shares as high risk in decreasing in value, and therefore too risky to insure. One of the major advantages of property investing is that it is insurable against most types of loss. This gives certainty and confidence for the investor to know that they will not lose the value of that investment should something unforseen happen. This is unusual among most types of investments, as they are subject to a much greater risk of loss. This is one reason that so many wealthy people hold most of their money in real estate. It is subject to much less risk than investments in the open market.

DEPENDABLE AND CONSISTENT CAPITAL GROWTH

CAPITAL APPRECIATION OF residential property in Australia has tracked, on average, at 8 per cent growth per year. This means that the value of investment property doubles every seven to ten years. This growth is dependable, and adds to the investor's wealth each and every year, compounding the value of the property. When this appreciation is combined with climbing rental rates over time, the return on investment is tremendous, and outpaces any other asset class.

YOU CAN USE THE BANK'S MONEY TO BUY

BECAUSE OF THE consistent capital appreciation of property, banks are willing to loan money on property. This is quite different from other investments where, at most, you might get a percentage of financing for a short period of time. This means that you can use relatively small amounts of your own money and leverage that cash to its maximum advantage, buying multiple properties and financing each one. As in the example of Fiona and Adam in the previous chapter, who borrowed money to buy multiple properties according to their risk tolerance, you can see the tremendous advantage this gives the investor by allowing them to accumulate wealth at a much faster pace than through other avenues.

YOU CAN INCREASE THE VALUE OF THE INVESTMENT

OFTEN WHEN ONE invests in shares or other investments, there is no further direct involvement. It doesn't really matter what you do or don't do; the investment is subject to market conditions that are out of your control. This is not true with property. You can take it upon yourself to negotiate a discount when buying, and then add additional value through renovation or refurbishment. This can give you an immediate return on your investment, rather than having to wait for it to grow in value. I frequently find properties that can be bought for 20 per cent or more below the current market price, due to a motivated seller. A refurbishment can easily add 10 to 15 per cent to a property. If both of these are combined, then the investor can buy a discounted property, refurbish it, and see an immediate gain in the value of that investment of 30 per cent or better. Another option to increase potential returns may simply be installing additional facilities into your property, like an air conditioning unit, and achieving an extra 5 to 10 per cent a week in rental return.

GENEROUS TAX DEDUCTIONS AND BENEFITS

THERE ARE NUMEROUS tax deductions and benefits available to the property investor that are not available to those who invest in other areas. Management fees, everyday expenses, maintenance costs, and many other items are considered deductible as expenses. Depreciation and interest expenses are also fabulous tools for increasing gain through the use of deductions available to the property investor. Any losses from negative cash flow on properties (negative gearing) may also be used to offset other income. It is very important to contact a tax accountant, who can help you maximise the available deductions and tax offsets.

PROPERTY IS CONSISTENT AND GIVES YOU CONTROL

ONE ITEM THAT helps property investors sleep at night is the fact that property does not have large and sudden swings in value, as some other investments do. You will not go to bed one night and wake up the next morning to find your investment worth only half what you paid for it, as some shareholders have.

You also have ultimate control over what happens to your property, and how much value you gain from the investment. This means you make all the decisions, rather than some executives thousands of miles away, whom you don't know and can't influence. You decide what happens to your investment and how much you will eventually gain.

CHAPTER 2
MY QUESTION

1. There are only three ways to make money: working, saving, and investing.

2. Property allows the investor to use leverage to gain wealth much faster and more easily than other investments.

3. Property can be insured against most types of loss, unlike other investments.

4. Property investing offers dependable and consistent capital growth.

5. Banks are very agreeable to loaning money on property because it is low risk.

6. You can instantly gain value by negotiating a discount and adding value to the property.

7. Property investors can take advantage of numerous tax deductions and benefits.

8. Property gives you ultimate control over your investment.

MY QUESTION: WHY INVEST IN PROPERTY?

MY ACTION PLAN AND NOTES

_____

_____

_____

_____

_____

_____

_____

_____

_____

_____

_____

MY CHOICE:

WHAT TYPE OF PROPERTY

SHOULD I INVEST IN?

CHAPTER 3

MY CHOICE:
WHAT TYPE OF PROPERTY SHOULD
I INVEST IN?

When you have to make a choice and you don't make it,
that itself is a choice.
– William James (1842 – 1910),
American Psychologist and Philosopher

WHO SAYS I WANT TO BE WEALTHY?

When I talk of creating wealth, it's not unusual for someone to ask this question. Wealth is not about accumulating wads of money – it's about creating freedom from worry, stress, and fear. Wealth is also about living how you want, having the freedom to choose how you spend your time with those you love, and not feeling forced to work at a job you don't particularly like. To want wealth for these purposes is not bad; in fact, it is the opposite, and can motivate you to take action. You may not feel that you really need to invest, but let me ask if you have ever dealt with any of the following worries:

- Do you and your spouse ever quarrel about money? Many experts believe that 90 per cent of divorces are due to financial challenges.

- Are you burdened with debt? Many people earn barely enough to cover minimum payments on their debt.

- Do you ever hide bills because you are ashamed, or dread opening them?

- Do you ever only pay the minimum payment on your ever-growing credit card balances?

- How much savings do you have? The life savings of the average person is less than $4000.

- How much have you earned so far in your lifetime? What do you have to show for it?

- Are you and/or your spouse working so much that you have to hire someone to care for your children?

- Can you afford a university education for all your children? Or for even one of them?

- What would you live on if you and/or your spouse lost your job?

- What would you do if someone in your family had sudden health challenges or were involved in a serious accident?

- Is money a daily struggle? Is it so tight that any unexpected expense is a burden to your family?

- Do you pray that the hot water service/car/refrigerator will last a bit longer because you have no idea how to pay for it when it fails?

- Do you say, 'I'll get another 1000 km out of my balding tyres'?

IF ANY OF these concerns are some that you have worried about, then you are not alone. However, it is a sad truth that if you continue on your present path, not only will you never achieve wealth or freedom, but financial ruin is a real possibility. Many people live dangerously close to financial disaster every day, and yet they don't have to! By taking small steps now to invest in assets that produce cash flow and appreciation, these worries could be a distant memory.

After a relationship break-up, I went through a near financial disaster. I was in a situation in which I would literally live on my last five dollars each week. I was emotionally distressed and basically just survived until I became stronger mentally. I lived a very basic life of going to work and coming home. All my bills were paid, but I did not even have enough money to buy a coffee out with a friend.

After living like this for approximately six months, I learned how to budget extremely well. I was living in Melbourne, and I wanted to move to the Gold Coast. I decided to take control of my life, and I set many goals that were focused on improving my situation. One day, I found a job on the Internet for a real estate office in Brisbane. From applying for the job to actually moving to Queensland was only a ten-day period. I literally had $200 in the bank when I drove to Brisbane. I had one friend in Brisbane whom I phoned to ask if I could stay with for a few weeks.

Thankfully, he was happy to help. I ended up staying for three weeks, and then I rented a one-bedroom, furnished unit on the Gold Coast. I started my new job, which paid $20,000 more a year than my previous job, but I had learned to live on much less. I remained on my same budget, and within a matter of months had saved enough money for a small deposit on a property. I found a small unit that was forty-two square metres in size (it was actually a holiday hotel room) for $70,000, and I decided it was cheaper to buy this and pay the loan rather than rent at $250 per week, as I would also gain any capital growth that accumulated on the unit. This unit was the smallest place you could imagine, but it was mine, and it was affordable.

It is not what happens that determines the major part of your future. What happens, happens to us all. It is what you do about what happens that counts.
– Jim Rohn, Business Philosopher

AFTER PURCHASING THE unit, I felt great pride. It was one of the best decisions I ever made. By living in this unit, I was able to buy a number of four-bedroom houses that I rented to tenants. I would often smile to myself that here I was, living in a unit that would fit in one of my tenant's lounge rooms. I lived in this unit for approximately eighteen months, and although I don't like to say that I sacrificed my living arrangements to get ahead, I did comprise on living in order to start building my property portfolio, which would make my life easier as I got older.

Even for those who consider themselves relatively well off, most have a long list of things they'd love to do when they retire, such as:

- Travel

- Visit the grandkids

- Go back to school

- Move to a beachside location

- Start a small business

- Play golf

- Buy a boat and fish

- Buy a holiday home

- Buy your dream vehicle

NO MATTER WHAT your personal dreams may be, they will take money, and while your goal may not be to become a multimillionaire mogul, being able to choose how you live is priceless. The key is to take control of your money and your life right now, rather than wait for your life to be controlled by your lack of money. You don't need thousands to get started, and as long as you have a plan, you will be amazed at what you can accomplish.

One of the greatest misconceptions people have about getting into property investment is that you must already be wealthy. Statistically in Australia, over 70 per cent of property investors earn incomes between $35,000 and $40,000 per annum, and over 90 per cent of all millionaires earned their money through investment in real estate. There is no limit to what you can earn, and if you are committed to becoming a property investor, you can be the millionaire next door that no one suspects!

Often people ask about investing in additional money in superannuation, share, or other investment vehicles prior to taking up property investment. Though these avenues get more time in the media, real estate can offer much greater returns. The reason for this is that you make money using two avenues in property investing, and most other investments just have one avenue for making money. For example, if you invested in shares and earned 8 to 10 per cent, you might consider that really good. Rental property earns both a percentage increase of, say, 8 to 15 per cent per year in value or capital growth, and a 10 to 15 per cent increase in rental income – and don't forget those tax credit advantages! This means that your investment could be earning 18 to 30 per cent per year, not even considering the deductions for expenses you incur for maintenance or bank interest.

If you have purchased a home, then you probably had to hand over a 20 per cent deposit, and you needed to have enough income to cover the payment each month. However, this is not the case with investment property, and many potential investors don't realise it. There's also good news if you own your home for more than a couple of years – you probably have a good bit of equity available to cover any cash that you will need to purchase your first investment property. This is due to the fact that you will have started with at least 20 per cent equity, which you covered with your deposit. As the years pass, you pay off the loan and lower the amount of debt. At the same time, the property is increasing in value, which gives you more equity to work with.

There is no doubt that some property investments work much better than others, and you may even know people who had a bad experience investing in properties. If this is the case, usually these investors made one or several key mistakes that could have been avoided. Throughout this book, I will talk about some of the pitfalls you can avoid with just a bit of knowledge. I'll use examples that will help you structure a loan correctly, and choose properties with the most rental and appreciation potential. Remember, it's not that money can't be made in every area of real estate – it can. It's about getting the best possible return for your investment dollar.

You can never start too early to invest in real estate, and you can also never start too late. As more and more baby boomers approach retirement age, concern grows among them and their families that they might outlive their money. Because they were one of the first generations to widely use consumer debt (bank loans), and because they saved little compared to previous generations, this concern is quite valid. However, with property, you can still get ahead, even if you have already retired. Several years from now, you can enjoy a nice stream of income and a much larger asset base than you have now. The wonderful thing is that as you age, it grows. You don't have to do a thing to help it along. Property is actually an attractive investment for many retirees, as it is a solid asset with predictable returns – which can't be said of investing in shares or similar investments.

FEAR IS THE ENEMY

Nothing in life is to be feared. It is only to be understood.
– Marie Curie (1867 – 1934), French Physicist

ONE OF THE things that concern me is a statistic I once heard at a financial seminar: 20 per cent of the population holds 80 per cent of the money. And the 80 per cent of the population that doesn't have much money and basically lives on what they earn (or less) does nothing to improve their situations. Why? I believe it is out of fear. Many would rather suffer their circumstances rather than risk making a wrong decision.

As I mentioned earlier in this chapter, I had nearly nothing when I started investing, and I can say that I had more than a few fears, but my desire to change my circumstances and my ambition to not be part of the 80 per cent who live on what they earn was stronger than my fear. My strength to overcome my fears came from reading personal development and motivation books. I would read Bob Proctor's book, *You Were Born Rich*, finish it one night, and then start it again the next. I did this for months on end.

Even the ones who toy with the idea of investing in property merely consider the idea, and then toss it aside out of indifference, with the thought that it will take too much effort. How much effort are you willing to put in to secure your future? When you think about the fact that most people get up and go to work for at least eight hours every day, not knowing if that job will be there tomorrow, how can you not justify a bit of time each evening or on the weekend to learn about property investment?

Few people have a definite and concrete plan for their future, but you can make one now. In the following chapters, I will detail how to set your goals and get the help you need to achieve what you want from life. There is no room for doubt or fear. Everyone started as a beginner at one point or another! The advantage you have is that there are so many people who can and want to help you along the way. These are other investors and real estate professionals who can guide and direct you, and don't think they are just in it for a dollar.

Real estate is set up on a commission basis for most of the professionals involved. They have a vested interest in making sure that you make more money and continue to invest, or they cease to make money. Other real estate investors are also frequently looking for partners or associates to pool their money with. Here again, if you don't make money, neither do they, and you get the benefit of their experience and knowledge.

Property investment can also provide a great source of pride and personal achievement. Remember when you bought your first home? Didn't you walk around the yard for a time with a grin on your face? I know I did! There's a thrill about owning a tangible piece of land to call your very own. Imagine that same feeling once you own two or five or fifty properties. Wouldn't you love to be able to drive down the street one day and say, 'I own that one, and that one and … well, I own the whole wonderful street!' Nothing makes you feel prouder than to point to a property and say, 'That's mine'.

Achieving starts with believing.

– Anonymous

SO WHICH TYPE of property is best to invest in? In the following, I list the types of investment properties and the differences between these properties.

CHOOSE YOUR PATH

PROPERTY INVESTMENT ALLOWS you to specialise in many different areas. I often recommend that investors do specialise because it is easier to become an expert in one area than to try to learn everything. You have numerous options, and I'll give you a quick list, but it is by no means comprehensive. Each area of property investment has unique features that you might choose to make your own.

LAND AND DEVELOPMENT

FEW PEOPLE REALISE that the main appreciation from property investment comes from land – not the structure that sits on it. For this reason, it is not uncommon for vacant land to grow much higher in value than a unit or apartment would. The reason for this is that the unit or apartment is actually allotted a small portion of the land that the building sits upon, as it has to be shared with all the unit owners, and so it doesn't have the capacity to appreciate at the same rate as, say, a single dwelling home with its own plot of land. This is not to say that apartments are not valid investments – they are – but there are other investments that have a higher potential for appreciation.

For the most part, vacant land isn't all that great an investment as it has no cash flow but still has expenses that must be paid, such as taxes and insurance. The one exception to this is if the land is adjacent to an area that is expanding or in the future path of progress. In this case, these nearby properties raise the value of the vacant property.

COMMERCIAL PROPERTY

COMMERCIAL PROPERTY CONSISTS of shops, stores, and offices. These properties can produce excellent income for an investor who is willing to learn the ins and outs. For the beginning investor, it may be an area to simply study and then eventually go back to at a later point. This is because commercial property typically involves a very large investment. It also usually requires the services of a professional management company as well. This is not something a first-time investor would usually be able to navigate alone, and can be intimidating even for an experienced investor.

One of the main differences between commercial property and residential is that commercial properties are not necessarily priced on any kind of inherent value. Their price and value are based on the income they produce in the form of rent. This means that there can be two identical buildings, one with no tenants and one that is fully rented. They will have vastly different values, even though they are identical. One way to determine this value, and thus the price you should pay, is to find the capitalised value. This is done by taking the total amount of yearly rents – for example, $200,000 – and dividing that by the yield or return you are seeking – in this example, 10 per cent. The formula would look something like this:

Rent / Yield = Capitalised Value

$200,000 / .10 = $2,000,000

But what if the same building next door was rented for $250,000? Then the value would be calculated as follows:

Rent / Yield = Capitalised Value

$250,000 /.10 = $2,500,000

This produces a drastic difference in the value of the property.

Commercial property also differs in that the tenants pay all outgoings or expenses, unlike residential, where the owner pays outgoings. As shown in our examples, the value of commercial property can vary wildly, and for this reason, it can often be bought at a significant discount, especially if it is not fully rented.

The downside is that, due to the fluctuations of commercial property, banks don't loan as high a percentage of the value – often only 60 to 70 per cent, rather than 80 to 100 per cent of its value.

RESIDENTIAL HOUSES

MOST SMALL OR novice investors find this market very lucrative and inviting. Many of us live in single dwelling homes, and the buying process is simple. There is also a vast array of homes that investors can buy in almost any area that may make good assets. For this reason, the vast majority of investors use single-dwelling homes as their investment of choice. It is also the one I will concentrate most on throughout the rest of this book.

Most of these types of properties will be located in the suburbs or in towns surrounding metropolitan areas. It is important to note that when looking for this type of property, it is very different from finding a home of your own. Your home reflects your personal needs and tastes, and it is unique and specific to you. The best investment properties are those that appeal to a large segment of the market rather than to your specific needs. For example, a one-room, one-bathroom house has a much smaller possible tenant pool than a three-bedroom, two-bathroom home does. It is best to select those properties that allow for quick and easy rental, and have a large tenant base.

It is also important that it be near transportation, good schools, and shopping. Your property should be in a neighbourhood that has a certain element of personal safety, and the home should be well maintained.

RESIDENTIAL UNITS AND FLATS

UNITS AND FLATS can also be purchased, but on the whole, they are much less satisfying from a monetary perspective. Since they have little land associated with them, they tend to appreciate at a much slower rate than single-family homes. While they are not necessarily to be avoided, you must exercise utmost caution when looking at them from an investment standpoint. You want to choose those units that have the most possibility for appreciation, such as penthouses or units with spectacular views.

HOLIDAY HOMES

PURCHASING A HOLIDAY home is much less about cash flow and more about lifestyle. Many people purchase a holiday home for their personal use, and then let that home when they are not on the property. This allows them to capture some of the expense of the home, while still retaining its use. This is a great way to purchase a home in an area in which you are planning to retire, well in advance of your actual retirement, and see if it really suits your future lifestyle, while allowing it to create some income on the side.

RENOVATION

MANY INVESTORS LIKE to take on property that needs work, renovate the property, and make a quick gain. This is great if you have skills that allow you to effectively complete these projects. Unfortunately, most of us don't have these skills, and even if you do, it can often be a risky proposition. That being said, there are numerous investors who stick to this one type of real estate transaction and avoid any issues with tenants all together. But a word of caution when markets are hot: some buyers are caught paying top dollar for properties that require extensive renovations when they could have purchased a fully renovated property for a similar amount.

AUCTIONS

THESE DAYS, REAL estate auctions have become more popular than reality TV! The drama of buying and selling large assets is quite exciting, and many people attend these sales just for the adrenalin rush. The great advantage of these auctions for the investor is that you can frequently find an excellent deal. However, they can be a little intimidating the first few times you give it a try. It is usually a good practice to attend several auctions before participating in one so you learn the basics. This also allows you to find someone at one of these auctions who can help you with the ins and outs.

Properties are auctioned for a number of reasons. Sometimes, the owner needs a quick sale and is willing to take the risk of an auction rather than wait months for an offer. Auctions are often the result of deaths, unexpected circumstances, or bank foreclosures, as auctions are considered the most accurate way of determining true property value. No matter the reason, great deals can be had if you are willing to look for them. The main point to remember with auctions is that you will need your financing preapproved.

Creating wealth through property investment is a process that takes a bit of planning and willingness to learn, but more importantly, it requires that you believe you can do it. You must have the patience with yourself to set out on the journey, and not be afraid of making a mistake.

CHAPTER 3
MY CHOICE

1. Fear can keep you in the life you have always known, but wealth awaits you if you invest in property.

2. Commercial property takes more of an investment, and its value is determined by rental income, not intrinsic value.

3. Most small or novice investors begin with residential properties.

4. Vacant land isn't a great investment unless it is adjacent to an area of growth.

5. Flats require caution from investors since they don't appreciate as quickly as single-family homes.

6. Holiday homes can allow you to own property in a location where you will later retire, and will also provide cash flow when you are not there.

7. Auctions have become a source of excitement and entertainment for many, but can also be a place to find a good deal.

MY ACTION PLAN AND NOTES

_____

_____

_____

_____

_____

_____

_____

_____

_____

_____

_____

_____

CHAPTER

4

MY MONEY PLAN:

HOW TO FIND THE BEST FUNDING

FOR MY PROPERTY PURCHASE

CHAPTER 4

MY MONEY PLAN:
HOW TO FIND THE BEST FUNDING FOR
MY PROPERTY PURCHASE

At least 80% of millionaires are self made. That is, they started with nothing but ambition and energy, the same way most of us start.
– Brian Tracy, American Business Philosopher

N ow, time to get to it. The real reason most people fear property investment is that they generally can't figure out where the money will come from to accomplish it. Many also fear a large amount of debt. While these things must be considered, they are not roadblocks. If you continually think that there is no way you will ever find a way to invest in properties, or any other investment for that matter, then you won't. There is an old saying that, 'The answer to great questions are only given to those who seek'.

The secret as to why the wealthy get wealthier is debt. They use other people's money to accumulate assets, which in turn creates huge capital growth and enormous wealth. There you go. It is not really any great secret, but many people are not aware of this. In this chapter, let me show you how to make debt your friend.

Now, there is such a thing as good debt and bad debt. You have heard your parents or friends talk about using cash to buy a TV, furniture, or the other toys we enjoy in our lives. The reason to use cash is because these items all depreciate or devalue in time. Bad debt is loan money that we take out to buy items that decrease in value. On the other hand, good debt is loan money we take out to purchase items that grow in value, such as property.

Think about what you want funding for and decide if it is good or bad debt and decide whether it will be a good or bad investment.

Our minds are powerful instruments, and they take in thousands of thoughts and images every day. Most of this is done on autopilot. When was the last time you got in the car and drove to work, and then realised you remembered virtually nothing about the drive? If we stopped and actively thought about every single image that crossed our path or every idea that popped into our heads, we'd never get anywhere! So, we have a screening system in our conscious minds. Our minds assume that whatever we focus upon or think about repeatedly is important. In turn, our minds bring related ideas and images to the surface.

If you want to be successful, it's just this simple:
Know what you're doing. Love what you're doing.
And believe in what you're doing.
– Will Rogers (1879 – 1935)

IF YOU USE this idea for investment and property management, you will quickly see what I mean. Once you focus on learning, and start reading up and looking around your neighbourhood for investments, help seems to come literally out of the woodwork. You will meet other investors, real estate professionals, and friends of friends who are in the business. While this may seem overwhelming at first, you soon realise that they were always there, but because you never focused your mind on property, you just didn't see them.

In fact, I'll guarantee as you are reading the pages of this book, your mind is absorbing the principles of investing in property. See if you don't soon meet some of that help that seems completely invisible right now!

YOUR CREDIT FILE

FOR MOST PEOPLE, it is an ugly yet mysterious idea that there is a file somewhere in cyberspace with their financial information. However, if you plan to invest in properties, it is important to know that this is, in fact, true. Your credit file lists personal details like your name, address, birth date, and driver's license number, and the list goes on. It also lists any defaults you have, which could include not paying any overdue invoices and any bankruptcy or judgments against you. Obviously, the importance of protecting your credit rating to a perfect standard is extremely important. As far as banks and mortgage brokers are concerned, you are your credit. They make decisions about whether to lend you money based on your ability to pay it back. While it's important to know where you stand in your borrowing ability, even if you have a few blemishes on your record, you have amazing control over how lenders view you.

Since different lenders put different weight on certain items in your file, discuss your credit with your broker and ask how to improve any deficiencies before you start looking for properties. Even if you don't have deficiencies, you may still be able to improve your credit. Why bother? Not only will it be easier to attain credit, but it will qualify you for better interest rates, which can add up to a great deal of money over the long term.

Subscribe to a credit reference company. These companies offer an annual service where they will notify you immediately of any changes to your credit history, such as defaults that are lodged against your name. They will also notify you of any person or company seeking information about your credit history. In addition, you can order a free copy of your credit file on the Internet. There are often frequent mistakes lodged against individuals due to events such as a death, divorce, or even a new live-in relative, which can cause things to appear in your file that are not yours. This is especially true if you share the exact same name as your parent or other relations.

As you continue to invest in property and pay on time, your credit will improve and your credit score will increase. However, it's important to understand that banks are a business. They are in business to make money, and they do that by assessing risk. It doesn't matter if you know you can make the payments on a property – they may disagree and turn you down. For this reason, it's good to think of them as part of the solution you may need, but not all of it.

This is one reason that you will often hear me talk about taking out a mortgage or line of credit in this book, and borrowing from multiple lenders that are both traditional and non-traditional. This spreads your risk around so that you don't have your entire portfolio tied to one financial institution. Often people think it is a good thing to have everything at one bank, but I disagree. Though the bank may treat you very well, they don't have to work for your business, and consequently you may not be getting all the bells and whistles that other investors receive. Many banks work on statistics that reveal that if a client has one product with their bank, they have a 10 per cent chance of keeping you as a client when you refinance, whereas if you have two products with them, they have a 89 per cent chance of retaining you as a client, and if you have three or more products of theirs, they have a 99 per cent chance of you remaining a client of their bank. Therefore, they do not need to offer established clients like yourself as much as a new client.

In addition, if all your banking is with one bank, this gives the bank too clear a financial snapshot of you. They know too much: which properties are currently rented and for how much, which properties are undergoing repairs, how much you have in savings, how much you make, and what you spend your money on.

It is my opinion that this constitutes too much power. It is difficult to weather a storm or setback if your lender is looking over your shoulder constantly. I find a partial financial picture is more than enough information for any one lender.

For the most part, to invest in real estate, you need at least some cash. You may be asking yourself, 'What about those no-money-down deals I hear about on TV?' No-money-down deals do exist. But that doesn't mean that cash isn't required at some point – it just means that you get all of your cash back by the close of the deal. Having said that, there are numerous other creative ways to increase your ability to buy homes, and we will discuss several of those. First, though, you need to know what to do to get started.

As I said before, you don't have to be wealthy or have loads of cash to get into real estate, but it helps if you have some. The way most individuals buy a home is to put down a deposit and then borrow the rest of the money necessary to complete the purchase. Most people refer to this as a standard or traditional purchase. This is only one option for purchasing property, and I always tell people that there are options open to you no matter what your financial situation or income bracket. Just realise that some of these options require much more work on your part. If you are willing to do that work, then you can soon be on your way, no matter if you own a mansion or a one-bedroom apartment. Creativity is the key, and the more options you consider, the more doors your mind will open to you.

So how big a deposit should you consider? It's really up to you, but as long as your rental income will produce a close to neutral or even positive cash flow, 20 per cent is great, if you are able. With a 20 per cent deposit, you avoid mortgage insurance with the bank. Mortgage insurance is not for your benefit – it is for the bank. Banks are able to insure your debt with their insurance company. The purpose of this is if you fail to meet your mortgage, then the mortgage insurance will cover your debt to the bank if they are forced to sell your property at a lower amount than the outstanding balance of your mortgage with the bank.

Many times, I have only put down a 5 to 10 per cent deposit, but it just means that I borrowed 90 to 95 per cent of the purchase price from the bank, which also means that the rental income did not cover the interest payment to the bank initially, and that I needed to add further money from my other income to meet the shortfall. I only ever borrow money from the bank as interest only (I never pay any of the principal off the loan). This keeps my monthly financial commitment lower, which in turns allows me to borrow more money in the future.

When considering how large a deposit to make, it is good to think of it as a trade off. The more money you put down on a property, the lower your interest rate. The less you put down, the higher the interest rate. This is because lenders assess interest rates based on risk. The more money you pay up front, the less they have to pay to have a claim to that asset, and the more likely it is that they will recoup that loss should you default. However, if the lender is asked to finance a very high percentage of the total loan, then that makes their risk of loss much higher should you default.

> *To become financially independent you must turn part of your income into capital; turn capital into enterprise; turn enterprise into profit; turn profit into investment; and turn investment into financial independence.*
> *— Jim Rohn, Business Philosopher*

MANY PEOPLE ARE aware that you can get loans for as much as 106 per cent of the value of the home. This allows you to buy the entire property, plus add any conveyance costs, stamp duty, and fees. The challenge is that you will probably pay a higher rate, but it can be feasible, especially in areas that are experiencing rapid capital growth.

If you are planning to hold the property for a number of years and want the best cash flow possible from the rent, then it makes more sense to put a little more down to get that better interest rate. However, if you are planning to have the property only a few years at the most, then you might want to hang on to as much cash as possible and pay a little higher interest in the short term.

SO WHAT DO you do if you are cash strapped and want to get around those high down payments? Here are several solutions:

1. We already touched on the equity in your home, but it is the easiest and most readily available source of cash for most people. The increased mortgage on your home is even more effective if your home is paid off

or nearly so. Every bank has a LVR (loan to value ratio), and this is the maximum they will loan out against a property. If your bank's LVR is 90 per cent, and you have a $300,000 home that you only owe $30,000 on, they will allow you to have a line of credit or increased mortgage of $240,000. Having this large lump sum allows you to do something unique – you can offer sellers below-market value that is quite attractive if the seller is in a hurry or is financially challenged. If you are then able to purchase the next $300,000 home at the discounted rate of $270,000, within a short time, the bank will value the home at the market price of $300,000 – which will give you an additional $30,000 equity that you didn't have before.

2. I would suggest if you had a large amount of equity in your home, say, in excess of $80,000, that you divide this amount up and look at buying a few properties, using the minimum amount that the bank will accept. I would recommend, if you plan to buy a couple of properties, that you buy the first one and see how you manage for a month or so, and then buy the second property, and so on. I always know all my facts before purchasing a property; for instance, how much the fees, stamp duty, and mortgage repayments are, and how much rent the property will achieve. But sometimes it is a great idea to settle into one property at a time, especially if it is your first or second.

3. There is computer software available today that will allow you to enter all your income and expenses, as well as forecast the growth of the rental income and property value in coming years. These types of programs are excellent for completing a full presentation of each property you own or buy. The programs will allow you to print report after report, enabling you to create an impressive document to submit to a lender. This shows you know what you are talking about in regards to budgeting and wealth creation. One software product that I have used is PIA by Jan Somers. This is an excellent program that allows you to see all the facts and figures on paper.

4. Small can be beautiful, so look for lower-priced properties or ones that need some refurbishment. These will generally require a lower deposit, or have owners who are more willing to be flexible on price. You can

also look for properties that have the opportunity for an owner live-in/ rental arrangement. This could be an older home near a college that has been split into individual units, or even a duplex. You can live in one of the apartments while collecting rent on the others. One word of caution here is that a lender will be concerned if the property is too small. Most lenders will not loan money on a dwelling that is less than 40 square metres in size. For example, if you invest in a very small, one-bedroom home, size will limit the number and type of tenants who can offset your mortgage to singles or young married couples. These groups tend to be more transient and move more frequently than do families. This could increase your vacancy rate and create severely negative cash flow.

5. Set up your own self-managed Superannuation Fund, and then use this fund to allow you to purchase rental property – provided it is an outright purchase with no loan or a joint venture with another entity. This means either you must pay in full for the property or join a group of investors also using Superannuation Funds. Then you can pool your money for outright purchases. This allows money that would otherwise only earn a given rate the chance to earn both cash flow and appreciation. Ask your accountant's advice regarding what a self-managed super fund can and can't do.

6. Owner financing, or vendor financing, is much more flexible than anything you might get through a bank or mortgage company, and sellers are many times open to all kinds of creative ideas. Vendor financing is when the owner or seller of the property allows the buyer to either borrow some or all of the property price from them at a negotiated interest rate and payment terms. In other words, the seller of the property becomes the financier. Don't be afraid to go this route, as it may prove to be a perfect option for you. It also offers the investor the chance to continue to buy properties, even if they do have a slightly negative cash flow, which can scare off many lenders. As we discussed, the trade off for this kind of arrangement is usually a higher interest rate, but this is still a valid option. Many real estate investors start this way and later, as their credit file and cash position improves, they turn to more conventional financing to get better interest rates.

I never allow any difficulties. The great secret of being useful
and successful is to admit no difficulties.
– Sir George Gipps (1791 – 1847),
Former Governor of New South Wales

7. Increasing your savings is not especially thrilling, but it is fine to increase your savings and wait for the right time. Going on a financial diet for a few months is a good idea for most people, whether they are trying to get into property investment or not. Cash offers so many more options that many people prefer to save up a deposit and then get started, rather than increasing their mortgage – especially if they are first timers. However, I would caution you not to wait too long, because often the capital growth you achieve in a property can grow faster than any money you save. You are costing yourself potential income if you put things off. Many investors fall into this trap of waiting until the time is perfect. Unfortunately, it never is. There is no such thing as perfect timing, and striving for it will lead to frustration. Do you want to look back ten years from now and regret the opportunities you passed up by waiting? Or do you want to look back and see all that you've accomplished by bolstering your confidence and moving forward?

8. Sharing the costs of a property with a partner or partners can also be a great way to get into the business, especially if the people you are dealing with are experienced. When two or more people work together, they can afford to take advantage of the better financing situations, while spreading the risk equally among them. It is much easier to build a portfolio of properties faster by working together than by working alone. Other partners may also offer you the opportunity to get into different areas of real estate investment that are their particular specialties, such as off-the-plan development opportunities, holiday rentals, or commercial ventures. This allows you to focus on what you do best, and still make money on what they do best.

THESE ARE JUST a few simple strategies that help you acquire your first property. After you have accomplished this, you can move on to more advanced financing and leveraging strategies that we will talk about in a later chapter. For right now, we want you to understand that anyone in any financial situation has options for getting into the real estate investment market. Some may be easy and some a bit more difficult, but they are there.

TYPES OF LOANS

THERE ARE THREE main ways to borrow money: a variable-rate loan, a fixed-rate loan, or a split loan. There are also other methods available to borrow money that are not as well known – for example, lines of credit (LOC). These are becoming more popular because they offer flexibility to the borrower.

Variable-rate loans are called this because their interest rate is variable. The rate can change throughout the loan term due to economic changes. Interest is calculated on a daily basis and added to your balance each month. Most lenders will allow you the option to make your payments weekly, fortnightly, or monthly, depending on your initial agreement.

Fixed-rate loans are exactly what they sound like. They are at fixed interest rates for a period negotiated with the lender. Most are for periods between one and five years, and can generally be refixed after the period expires. The repayment for the period is a fixed rate, and most lenders will agree to a weekly, fortnightly, or monthly period.

Split loans are a combination of variable and fixed loans. For example, if you borrow $200,000, you could choose to fix $100,000 into a fixed rate and keep the other $100,000 variable. Some people decide to split loans to give themselves some certainty with their payments in case the interest rates increase. Obviously, no can know for certain what interest rates are going to do, so many borrowers feel this has the benefit of both worlds.

Lines of credits are an excellent method, but the borrower must be disciplined with their funds to manage their loans efficiently. Recently, I heard of the split revolving line of credit. The purpose of this is to split the loan into separate debts for properties owned or purchased into a tax-deductible and non tax-deductible loan. The principle is that the income received from a rental property is allocated against the principal place of residence loan (or the non tax-deductible loan), which enables the non tax-deductible debt to be paid off sooner and the repayments on the tax-deductible loan are paid by drawing down the line of credit against the rental property, thus allowing high tax deductibility and also reducing your non tax-deductible loan in a shorter time span.

Most loans can be either interest only or principal and interest payments. Interest only means that you never pay anything off the initial debt for the term of the loan. Principal and interest involves paying a portion of principal, as well as the lender's interest with every payment. Maximum loans are usually for thirty years, although with the ever-competitive money market, more and more lenders are increasing loan periods to make the repayments more affordable, and many other terms are more negotiable these days between lenders.

As previously mentioned in this chapter, you will find lenders are more negotiable if there is an opportunity for them to secure more than one loan with you, or for them to refinance all your loans. However, although this initially may give you more power to get what you want, the lender may have too much control afterwards.

Initially, looking at financing a property can be quite daunting, and I would recommend you start with a mortgage broker rather than by working directly with banks. A broker has the ability to determine upfront which lender will meet your requirements the easiest and the fastest. A word of advice: find a broker who is also an investor. I work on this theory for most professionals I deal with, as I want to work with people who know and understand the pros and cons of being an investor. Most brokers are paid a commission from the lenders for securing your loan through them.

Another main reason for dealing with a broker who is an investor is that he or she will guide you better into a loan structure that will protect your assets against possible problems that may occur with one property. It is important to keep your properties separate from one another to prevent risking any properties against another. For example, if you ever default on a property loan and the bank or lender decides to sell your property to recoup their outstanding interest owed, you do not want the lender to come after any of your other properties or assets. It is imperative that you do not cross collateralise your loans. Cross collateralisation is when you have more than one property secured against one loan. The consequences of this is that if you have used a property as security for the lender to buy another property and you default for any reason on one of these loans, the lender has the ability to sell the defaulted property without your consent. If that lender sells one of your properties and does not receive the amount you owe, they have the authority to sell your other property to recoup the outstanding money you owe. The reason the lender is able to do this is because you gave them authority when you crossed collateralised that, if you fail to pay one loan, guarantees the other property against the debt. It is very important to set up loan structure correctly, and I highly recommend that you seek expert advice on this matter.

HOW TO APPLY FOR A LOAN

WHEN YOU SUBMIT an application to a lender, you will be required to complete their application form. If you use a finance broker, this process will be a lot easier, as a broker generally will help you complete this. You will be required to provide evidence of your financial situation. The types of documents you will need to include are

- Personal identification evidence, such as a driver's license or passport
- Recent pay slips
- A letter from your employer
- Rental statements for any existing investment properties
- Share statements of dividends

- A group certificate

- Tax returns

- Bank statements showing any savings

- Statements of other loans

- Credit card statements

THE LENDER APPLICATION form will ask you to fill in an asset and liability statement. The purpose of this statement is to prove to the lender that you meet their lending criteria and can substantiate the loan. An asset and liability statement will ask the following:

Details	Amount per Month	Total
Income		
Salary/Wage		
Overtime		
Car Allowance		
Commissions		
Rental Property Income		
Shares Income		
Other Income		

Details	Amount per Month	Total
Assets		
Own Property		
Vehicles		
Investment Properties		
Shares		
Superannuation		
Savings		
Liabilities / Expenses		
Rent/Mortgage		
Car Lease/Loan		
Credit Cards		
Personal Loan		
Child Support		
Other Debt		

Using a finance broker will generally take some of the stress out of applying for a loan. The broker will help you with all the requirements the bank needs and will usually explain lending terms in language that is easy to understand.

Finally, I suggest that when you find a brilliant broker, you hang on to him or her. Brilliant brokers are worth their weight in gold.

CHAPTER 4
MY MONEY PLAN

1. The secret to why the wealthy get wealthier is the constructive use of debt.

2. Cash can allow you to get better deals and better interest rates.

3. You must understand all different types of loans and financing to meet your goals.

4. The LVR (loan value ratio) ratio will determine how much the bank will loan on a particular property.

5. Variable loans have a variable interest rate, and are suitable if you plan to have the investment for just a few years.

6. Fixed-rate loans have a fixed interest rate, and are more suitable for longer-term investments.

7. Find a mortgage broker who is also an investor to guide you to the correct loan structure for you.

MY ACTION PLAN AND NOTES

_____

_____

_____

_____

_____

_____

_____

_____

_____

_____

_____

CHAPTER

5

MY POWER TEAM:

HOW TO SURROUND MYSELF WITH

PRICELESS ADVICE

MY POWER TEAM:
HOW TO SURROUND MYSELF WITH
PRICELESS ADVICE

Be with wise men and become wise.
– Proverbs 13:20

I t's not unusual for people to start getting bogged down in financial information about now. Once you start to understand financing and are ready to look for properties, you will need a team of professionals to get through all the technicalities, contract specifics, and available options. It's not unusual to be nervous about this stage. You're not an expert yet, but you will be, and the confidence will follow. Remember, the hardest property to buy is your first one.

Even if you're great at figuring out cash flows and tax strategies, you still may suffer from the inability to make the final decision to purchase. Property is a big investment, and no one wants to make a mistake. It's times like these when good mentors are invaluable. They are experienced, understand where you are (they've been there too), and can offer sound advice and encouragement.

As you get the message out to family and friends, other investors will gravitate toward you. It's a natural phenomena that like seeks out like. Investors remember what it was like to be brand new, and want to impart their wisdom. Many of them were helped along the path to successful property investment and want to give back. Let them, and talk to everyone you can.

Talk to professionals in the business and to individuals who have made money in real estate – or even lost money. Try to talk to those who have owned property for years, and to those who have recently started in the business. You will find that everyone has a unique and interesting story to tell, and you can learn from them all.

All of these people will shorten your learning curve and make things easier for you. Not only will they tell you what to do, they will also tell you what not to do, which can be much more valuable. You will also see that each individual has a different idea of what he or she want out of their investment and how far they want to go. Some want to become major property owners, and some don't.

As you talk to people who are experienced and have been in the business for any length of time, you will come across those who have lost money and who have failed. While I hope their comments don't discourage you, I do hope they do serve to provide the awareness that, just like any other kind of investment, real estate can lose money if not handled properly. Sometimes it is easy to lose sight of that when the market is booming, but you must be aware that due diligence and good business practices are your best friends.

The best people to talk to are people who are doing what you want to do. If you want to specialise in refurbishments, talk to people who actively do that. Pick their brains and see if that's really the right direction for you. If you want to get into trading property, then find someone who specialises in that area. How? There are many ways.

Knowledge is power.
– Francis Bacon (1561 – 1626), English Philosopher

Professionals, such as realtors, accountants, lawyers, and even other people you meet through networking groups, who work within the real estate investment area can recommend clients or individuals they know who would be willing to talk to you. These professionals can become invaluable members of your team as you build your business.

ASSEMBLING YOUR TEAM

AS YOU TALK to property investors, you will also want to talk to and find some key professionals to advise you in other areas. Things like taxes, insurance, and legal liability are areas that must be addressed, and getting advice from experts in these fields will save you many dollars down the road.

It is important to find professionals to work with before you start purchasing property. These professionals can help you avoid costly mistakes, and can also help you understand the taxes and legal implications up front.

One of the first professionals you consult should be an accountant who is familiar with property investing. While you may have been told or heard that properties are a great tax deduction, this may or may not be true for you – or at least not as good if you do not receive the right advice. A good accountant will ask for a personal balance sheet, which includes all of your assets and liabilities. He or she will also ask about your income and current obligations. By evaluating your entire income and asset structure, your accountant can tell you what your tax considerations will be, depending on which area of real estate investment you wish to engage in. This reduces the chances of a nasty surprise from the tax office later on, and may influence your decision as to which type of real estate investment you want to engage in, or the financial structure of how you want to purchase property.

One item that is of particular importance in the area of tax deductions is depreciation. It is a great help to obtain a depreciation schedule from an ATO-recognised, qualified expert. Accountants can only calculate the allowable depreciation if they know the purchase price of the item, but they are frequently unqualified to calculate the age or installation cost of an item a previous owner installed. This may sound like a small thing, but it can add up to big dollars, as depreciation has a direct effect on your overall investment return, especially if you purchase older properties that have been renovated.

One of the most important professionals you will deal with is a real estate sales agent. These individuals are often the first to hear of new and promising properties that come on the market. It is important to find a sales agent you work well with and can trust. Talk with this person about the type, price range, and condition of properties you seek. This will keep you from having to hunt for properties or drive all over town, and allow you to maximise your time attending to other areas of your business. The seller pays the sales agent a commission when the deal is finished. They can provide high quality photos of potential properties for investment, and also help you sell properties from your portfolio as the need arises.

Finding a qualified sales agent who understands exactly the kind of investing you wish to do can take some time, but it is well worth it. A good place to start is to get recommendations from other investors, friends, or professionals, and then make appointments with those agents. In short, you should look for a real estate agent who is a full-time professional with an excellent reputation for honesty and integrity. If possible, you also want someone who is an expert, not only about the geographical marketplace, but also about the type of investment property you are looking for.

Personally, when I am looking for investment properties in areas that are new, I look for an agent who is also an investor. I ask the agent if he or she owns any investment properties, as I find that these agents understand what I am looking for. For years, working in real estate, I have regularly received calls from investors, both interstate and overseas, who are looking for property in the areas I cover. These people do not know me, my reputation, or whether I am an investor. I tell them that I am an investor myself, and this tells the investor that I understand what they need. There are many properties I have sold over the years that I would call good owner-occupier properties, and others that I would call great investment properties. There is a difference, but many agents miss this when they are not investors themselves.

When I find a property that would make for a fantastic investment property, I often make a call to one of my clients. Because I am an investor myself, I've always been able to provide the information the investor needs: the age of the property, rental return, infrastructure, future development planned, forecasted capital growth from specialised researchers, and what they could do to increase the value of the property or the rental return.

One of my clients from Victoria wanted to purchase in Queensland. I was in touch with him initially, and then he flew to Queensland a month later. I showed him a few properties and advised him on a particular house that I felt made for a great investment. He purchased this property before flying home, and all was well. Within another three weeks, I had another property that was similar to the one he had purchased. I phoned him to tell him to buy this other property, as I could see what was happening in the market and I felt that this area was on the verge of good growth. He was on the line as far as being able to borrow further money. After a few weeks, all was well and the bank gave him the okay. Within three months of purchasing both these properties and taking my advice, he made in excess of 24 per cent of capital growth on the properties, and they were still rising.

There are other professionals out there who see the opportunity in the markets, and I would recommend listening to these people, getting their advice, asking for their reasons and evidence, and then making your decision.

The desire of knowledge, like the thirst of riches,
increases ever with the acquisition of it.
– Laurence Sterne (1713 – 68), British Writer and Clergy

IT IS ALSO very important, especially for the beginning investor, not to represent yourself as something that you are not. If you are new to the business, say so. Don't pretend that you're a pro. The agent will quickly see through the charade and will not take you as a serious investor. But a word of caution: the selling agent is employed by the sellers, and therefore is working for them. Even if the agent tells you to purchase a particular property, do your own research and check the facts yourself. You must also be honest with the agent as far as your budget. If you spend a great deal of time having the agent find the perfect investment, but then are unable to secure financing, you may have a difficult time working with that agent again. So, check out the financial aspects first, and see what the bank says about your ability to buy a property. The following diagrams show both the traditional method and the new method that I would suggest you use to buy property.

TRADITIONAL METHOD

Go to contract on a property

Get finance

Settle

Talk to accountant

MY METHOD

Talk to accountant

Get financing

Go to contract

Settle

COVER ALL YOUR bases before entering into any property contract. You have control of all your investments, so be sure that all your methods are to your best advantage.

Don't feel pressured by any agent to buy on the spot. Good deals come along every day, and often the reason for pressure is to get a house sold quickly so its defects are less likely to be noticed. This is another reason to choose an agent who is an investor, as he or she is less likely to unload a less-than-great property on you. An agent who is also an investor knows that you could be buying properties consistently for many years, and therefore will take great precautions to be sure that you start out with good ones.

When you meet with your potential real estate agent, you will want someone who is eager to communicate with you and keep you informed. The agent will also need to be a good fit for you, and be someone whom you are comfortable dealing with. The level of interpersonal skills a real estate agent must have cannot be underestimated. Your agent will be presenting offers and negotiating contracts on your behalf, so persistence and perseverance are very important. Once an agent gets to know you and your investment goals, he or she will think of you first when they hear of a new listing, and many times this allows you the first chance at a new property before it even goes on the listing service.

When I see a property that's for sale, I can usually think of a potential buyer. I have many clients who are repeat investors, who all have specific areas and features that they want in a property, and after years in the business, I know when I have listed a property whom the buyer is likely to be.

Your most valuable asset can be your willingness to persist longer than anyone else.
– Brian Tracy, Business Philosopher

ANOTHER REAL ESTATE professional who can assist you is a buyer's agent. The difference between a buyer's agent and a sales agent is that a buyer's agent works for you to achieve a maximum sales price, as opposed to working for the seller. Buyer's agents are a fantastic option for people who have limited time, who don't live in the area where they want to buy property, and who have previously established relationships with sales agents. Buyer's agents work for you, and can generally negotiate a great deal for a client. Obviously, you as the buyer pays for their services, so take into consideration the cost of their services. They usually charge a percentage of the sale, but remember: they may save you more in the overall deal if they have strong negotiating skills.

INSPECTIONS

WHEN YOU DO locate a property, either with or without an agent, you will want to have that property inspected by a licensed building inspector. The inspector will give you a report as to not only the structural integrity of the property, but also its aesthetic condition. The contract can be written on contingency or 'subject to' an acceptable inspection to protect you from any surprises. This will be done prior to settlement.

More people these days think of having a termite and pest inspection for an investment property, and this is important. Not only can termites and pests cause potential damage to the building, but they can also harass tenants to the point of litigation if the issue is not resolved. The inspector will take photos, and many inspectors today have an infrared video machine that can detect changes within the wall cavities that are due to termites. They document any damage done, or lack thereof, which will give you something to make a comparison with should you ever have a pest challenge.

If you have numerous properties, you will often have a property manager look at the potential purchase. The property manager will be the most knowledgeable on how to assign rental rates given the condition and arrangement of the property. He or she will also be able to give honest input on upkeep and management costs, and what you can do to improve rental potential and returns. Most sales agents are not property managers, so it is often a good idea to request an inspection from a manager who is not the sales agent for the property you are buying. This prevents a conflict of interest.

Most lenders will have a bank valuation inspection completed prior to settlement. This confirms that the price you paid is the fair market value. The lender normally commissions this.

CONVEYANCING

CONVEYANCING IS THE legal term used for property transactions, and includes checking all matters effecting the property. A solicitor or conveyancing clerk will handle conveyancing on a property, so it is important to find one you can work with on numerous properties. It is also good to consult with them regarding any potential liability and legal issues that could get in your way, such as tenant agreements and disputes.

Solicitors who specialise in conveyancing can provide you with nearly any contract special condition that you could need. A common contract condition that many buyers use is that 'the sale on the property is subject to a building and pest inspection and that the buyer is satisfied with the outcome'. A building and pest inspection is done to check that the house does not have termites eating it out and that it is structurally sound.

There are also books and DVDs available to buyers that are written specifically with all real estate clauses ever known. Rob Balanda has written numerous books on clauses and conditions that can be used for all real estate transactions and property purchasing contracts. These books could prove invaluable to you, as many clauses that are written into contracts by non-legal professionals can create further challenges if they are not written with all legalities taken into account. For example, if you buy a property subject to a building and pest inspection and only write on the contract 'subject to the buyer conducting a building and pest inspection' and fail to add the words 'to the satisfaction of the buyer' this may not allow you the option to withdraw from the contract if termites are found. You need to include the clause 'to the buyer's satisfaction'.

A clause that I have commonly seen absent from contracts is one that deals with situations where a buyer wants to settle on a property with vacant possession (no tenant in the property), when the property is currently occupied by a tenant. Herein can be the challenge: each state varies in tenancy legislation, but in general terms, most tenant legislation declares that a tenant is to leave a property in a fair and reasonably clean condition. But the challenge is to determine the meaning of 'fair and reasonable'.

I have experienced many a property handed over in a very poor state, but by the time an owner tried to pursue any compensation from the tenant through legal channels, the time and effort outweighed the compensation. What usually occurs in these situations is that the buyer has minimal chance of seeking compensation from the seller, and therefore settles on a property that requires up to $600 cleaning to be completed prior to anyone occupying the property. On properties that I have purchased with tenants vacating prior to settlement, I add a clause that states that the seller must present the property to me at settlement in a professionally clean manner, including professional carpet cleaning. I experienced this very situation with one property I purchased, and because I had the cleaning clause in this contract, I was able to refuse to settle until the seller rectified. What actually happened was that the seller compensated me financially for the cleaning and settlement still occurred on the set day.

In summary, one of my biggest recommendations that I can give you is to have a team of professionals supporting you. They have studied for years to achieve their qualifications, and you can have the benefit of their wisdom.

CHAPTER 5
MY POWER TEAM

1. In order to find the best properties, you must create a relationship with a real estate agent.

2. It is important to be honest with your sales agent and check out your finances first.

3. Inspections are a necessary part of the final sale, and contracts should be contingent on these inspections.

4. It is a very good idea to work with other professionals who are also investors, as they can point you in the right direction.

5. Listen to the professionals. They can provide a wealth of knowledge.

6. Be sure that important clauses are not left out of the contract.

MY ACTION PLAN AND NOTES

_____

_____

_____

_____

_____

_____

_____

_____

_____

_____

CHAPTER

6

MY BUSINESS PLAN:

CREATE THE PLAN AND

STRATEGY FOR FINANCIAL

SUCCESS

CHAPTER 6

MY BUSINESS PLAN:
CREATE THE PLAN AND STRATEGY
FOR FINANCIAL SUCCESS

Self-trust is the first secret of success.
– Ralph Waldo Emerson (1803 – 82),
American Essayist, Poet, and Philosopher

Y ou are now, in every sense of the phrase, a businessperson starting your investment plan. When investing, it is very important to consider what kind or type of business structure you want to use for your property investment. Most just assume they will have a one-person structure and keep it as simple as possible – which is fine, unless you get sued. We live in an incredibly litigious society, and being a landlord or property owner of any kind these days seems to invite litigation. This is an area that you should certainly consult a solicitor and accountant regarding, to determine the best possible structure for your future benefit based on your plans. Few wealthy people own anything – their assets are all held by trusts or corporations to protect them if they are personally sued. While it is a sad state of affairs, it is a sign of the times we live in, and something to be aware of.

Taxes are one of the main concerns when deciding on a business structure. For investors within Australia, there are four main business structures: sole trader, partnership, trust, or company. While only you can decide what is best for your situation, it is very important to choose correctly, and for this reason I recommend consulting a tax accountant prior to setting up your business. Most people start out as sole traders, and then alter the structure of their business as their needs dictate. Each type has its benefits and downsides, but you are not locked into any structure and you can change as your business grows. No matter which business structure you eventually choose, it is important to understand the taxation nuances that go with it. As a general rule, costs and complexity increase as you move from sole trade to partnership to a trust or company.

The following table is taken from the Australian Tax Office website, and is just an illustration of the taxation details that go with each structure. Please check the latest changes and laws with your tax accountant, as these charts are examples only.

Structure	Features
Sole trader	**Description:** A sole trader is the simplest business structure and consists of an individual trading on his or her own. That person controls and manages the business. **Tax file number:** A sole trader uses their individual tax file number when they lodge their income tax return. **ABN:** A sole trader who is carrying on an enterprise in Australia may apply for an ABN (Australian Business Number) from the Australian Taxation Office for their business and use this number for all their business dealings.

Structure	Features
Sole trader	**Who pays income tax:** The income of the business is treated as the person's individual income, and they are solely responsible for any tax payable by the business. This means that, after deducting allowable expenses, they include all their business income with any other income and report it on their individual tax return. Sole traders pay the same tax as individual taxpayers, according to the marginal tax rates. Individuals don't pay tax on the first $6,000 they earn. This is called the tax-free threshold. Sole traders generally pay PAYG (Pay As You Go), which is paying tax throughout the year which goes towards their end of year tax liability as determined by the Australian Taxation Office when you submit your tax return.
	GST: A sole trader who is carrying on an enterprise may apply for GST (Goods and Services Tax) registration. This can be applied for on the ABN application form. A sole trader is required to be registered for GST if their annual turnover is $75,000 or more ($50,000 or more prior to 1 July 2007).
	Drawings: A sole trader cannot claim a deduction for money they "draw" from their business. Amounts taken from a sole trader business, and regarded by some as their "wages," are not wages for tax purposes and are not tax-deductible.
	Personal services income: If you are a contractor or consultant, deductions in relation to this income may be treated differently.
	Superannuation: Sole traders are responsible for their own superannuation arrangements. They need to pay superannuation contributions for any employees they employ to help run the business.

Structure	Features
Partnership	**Description:** For tax purposes, a partnership is an association of people who carry on business as partners or receive income jointly. **Tax file number:** A partnership needs its own tax file number and uses it when lodging its annual income tax return. This can be applied for on the ABN application form. **ABN:** If the partnership is carrying on an enterprise in Australia, it may apply for an ABN and use this number for all the partnership's business dealings. **Who pays income tax:** A partnership is not a separate legal entity and doesn't pay income tax on the income earned by the partnership. Instead, each partner pays tax on their share of net partnership income. While the partnership doesn't pay tax, it does have to lodge an annual partnership income tax return to show all income earned by the partnership and deductions claimed for expenses incurred in carrying on the partnership business. The tax return also shows each partner's share of new partnership income. Partnerships are not liable to pay PAYG instalments. Instead, individual partners may be liable to pay PAYG instalments on their share of income from each partnership of which they are a member. **Drawings:** Partnerships cannot claim a deduction for money partners "draw" from their business. Amounts taken regularly from a partnership business, and regarded by some as their "wages," are not wages for tax purposes and are not tax-deductible. **GST:** Partners may apply for GST registration for the partnership if it is carrying on an enterprise. This can be applied for on the ABN application form. A partnership is required to be registered for GST if its annual turnover is $75,000 or more ($50,000 or more prior to 1 July 2007).

Structure	Features
Partnership	**Personal services income:** Income and deductions in relation to this income may be treated differently.
	Superannuation: Partners in a partnership are responsible for their own superannuation arrangements, as they are not employees of the partnership. But a partnership needs to pay superannuation contributions for other employees of the partnership.

Structure	Features
Trust	**Description:** A trust is an obligation imposed on a person to hold property or income for the benefit of others (who are known as beneficiaries).
	Tax file number: A trust must have its own tax file number and uses it when lodging its annual income tax return. The trustee needs to apply for a tax file number in its capacity as trustee of the trust. A tax file number can be applied for on the ABN application form.
	ABN: If the trust is carrying on an enterprise in Australia, the entity that is trustee may register for an ABN in its capacity as trustee of the trust.
	Who pays income tax: Whether or not a trust has a tax liability depends on the type of trust, the wording of its trust deed, and whether the income earned by the trust is distributed (in whole or in part) to its beneficiaries. Where the whole of the net trust income is distributed to adult resident beneficiaries, the trust will have no liability. Where all or part of the net trust income is distributed to either non-residents or minors, the trustee will be assessed on that share on behalf of the beneficiary. In this case, the beneficiary is required to declare that share of net trust income on their individual income tax return, and also claim a credit for the amount of tax liability paid on their behalf by the trustee.

Structure	Features
Trust	Where the net trust income is accumulated by the trust, the trustee will be assessed on that accumulated income at the highest individual marginal rate. If a trust is carrying on a business, each year all income earned by the trust and deductions claimed for expenses incurred in carrying on that business must be shown on a trust tax return. The tax return also shows the amount of income distributed to each beneficiary. Trusts are not liable to pay PAYG instalments. Instead, the beneficiaries or trustees may be liable to pay instalments. **GST:** If the trust is carrying on an enterprise, the entity that is trustee can register for GST in its capacity as trustee of the trust. This can be applied for on the ABN application form. A trust is required to be registered for GST if its annual turnover is $75,000 or more ($50,000 or more prior to 1 July 2007). The registration threshold for non-profit organisations is $150,000 ($100,000 prior to 1 July 2007). **Personal services income:** Income and deductions in relation to this income may be treated differently. **Superannuation:** Trusts may need to pay superannuation contributions for trustees if they are also employed by the trust. A trust also needs to pay superannuation contributions for other employees of the trust.

Structure	Features
Company	**Description:** An incorporated company is a distinct legal entity with its own income tax liability, separate from an individual's income tax. Companies are regulated by the Australian Securities and Investments Commission. A company is a more complex business structure, with set-up and administrative costs usually being higher than for other business structures.

Structure	Features
Company	A company is required to have a separate bank account. For tax purposes, a company means a body or association, incorporated or unincorporated, but does not include a partnership or a non-entity joint venture. **Tax file number:** A company needs to apply for a tax file number and uses it when lodging its annual income tax return. This can be applied for on the ABN application form. **ABN:** A company registered under the Corporations Act 2001 is entitled to an ABN. A company that is not registered under the Corporations Act may register for an ABN if it is carrying on an enterprise in Australia. **Who pays income tax:** If a business is run as a company, the money earned by the business belongs to the company. Under the self-assessment system, companies have to lodge an annual company tax return, which shows the income and deductions of the company and the company's income tax payable. Companies also usually pay PAYG instalments, which are credited against their annual income tax liability. A company pays income tax on its assessable income (profits) at the company tax rate, which is currently 30 per cent. The amount of tax to be paid is reduced by any PAYG instalments reported during the year. There is no tax-free threshold for companies. **GST:** A company may apply for GST registration if it is carrying on an enterprise. This can be applied for on the ABN application form. A company is required to be registered for GST if its annual turnover is $75,000 or more ($50,000 or more prior to 1 July 2007). The registration threshold for non-profit organisations is $150,000 ($100,000 prior to 1 July 2007).

Structure	Features
Company	**Personal services income:** Income and deductions in relation to this income may be treated differently. **Superannuation:** Companies need to pay superannuation contributions for all of their eligible employees, including company directors.

Source: Australian Taxation Office

IT IS ALSO important to seek legal counsel to understand the legal liabilities and ramifications of each type of business structure.

Another important area to have good advice in is insurance. As a landlord, you can get policies that cover damage to the property, but you can also get rental income coverage should something unfortunate happen. For example, let's say a tenant signs a twelve-month lease, and three months into the contract, the tenant falls behind in the rent. Upon chasing the tenant for arrears, you find that the tenant has actually left the property after causing malicious damage to the walls and carpeting. While you then embark on repairing the property and seeking a new tenant, you can have an insurance policy that will cover you for the loss of rent and the damage to the property, therefore ensuring that you recoup all your out-of-pocket expenses. This type of policy protects your cash flow and keeps you from suffering a loss of income.

As you transition from working for someone else to working for yourself as an independent businessperson, there will, of course, need to be some adjustments. Part of that comes with an adjustment of mindset to seeing yourself as a business owner. Property investing gives you credibility, and as you feel different about yourself and your abilities, people will respond and treat you more positively and with more respect.

One of the most difficult things for those making the transition to investor is the issue of time management. Juggling all of the responsibilities, especially early on while you are still working, can be intimidating and daunting. It is important from the very first day to treat your investing as a business. That doesn't mean that you pay attention for a few months and then slack off. You must be involved every single day, and it is a good idea for you to manage the first one or two properties you own. This will give you a feel for the number and frequency of issues that might arise and how they should be dealt with. It will also convince you of the value of a property manager.

The secret of success is constance to purpose.
– Benjamin Disraeli (1804 – 81),
Former British Prime Minister

AS YOU START out, plan to devote a specified, scheduled time to your real estate investing and portfolio. Constantly read and be aware of what is happening in the market. You can do this through books or subscriptions to property-investment magazines. You can also attend seminars to learn some of the latest ideas and techniques for acquiring properties.

While you shouldn't try to time the market, realise that life situations, circumstances, and normal occurrences, such as divorce, relocation, upsizing, and downsizing, never change in any market. Study and know the fundamentals of the property market, and timing will find you. If you have a specified time each day to focus on your business, there is less chance that you will miss the opportunities.

Your home office need not be fancy, but it does need to exist. The more you set yourself up as a businessperson, the more you will act like one. The essentials are a phone, fax, copier/printer, scanner, and computer with Internet access. Most people already have these basic elements. There are also numerous real estate software programs available that help with income and expense tracking, goal setting, and planning.

The bookkeeping aspect of managing your properties must be attended to regularly and diligently. If you do not carry a service contract on your appliances, and don't have someone handy whom you are comfortable with, you will find this to be a full-time job that will take time away from finding other investments, or simply from spending time with your family. Don't choose to be a handy hero. There are people you can pay to do this, and the work will be accomplished much more professionally and efficiently, without taking time away from the more important things in your life. Your time is valuable. Treat it as such.

SETTING BUSINESS GOALS

AT THE VERY beginning of this book, I asked you to create a wish list. Have you done this? I asked you to think about and envision what your life might be like. Now that you know that these dreams are not just wishes, and that you can really create that life for yourself through property investing, we are going to turn those wishes into achievable goals.

Goal setting can be like walking a tightrope. While you don't want to be set your goals so high as to be unattainable, you also don't want to set them too low. Otherwise, you will spend your life underachieving, and even if you reach every low goal you set, you will know it wasn't nearly as good as it could have been.

In order for a goal to be achieved, you must not only create it, but also believe it. Make no mistake – you will have to work for it, sacrifice, and be willing to put in 100 per cent, no matter what challenges you face. Remember: winners never quit, and quitters never win.

Writing down your business goals is an important part of that belief process. Though many people set goals once a year, at New Year's or on their birthdays, they often quietly place their goals in a drawer and don't even look at them until the next year. But even they are way ahead of everyone else. A good life takes active planning and participation, and even if you're the once-a-year kind of goal setter, that's better than nothing. But in order to move forward as quickly as possible, it pays to revisit your goals on a weekly and monthly basis. Then, at the end of the year, you can be pleasantly shocked at how far you've come in such a short time, rather than feeling depressed at having the same exact goals for the next year because you didn't accomplish anything.

If you go to work on your goals, your goals will go to work on you. If you go to work on your plan, your plan will go to work on you. Whatever good things we build end up building us.
– Jim Rohn, Business Philosopher

IT IS IMPORTANT to be able to articulate what you want from your property investment business it and to write it in such a way as to be achievable. An effective goal has certain identifiable elements. A good goal is

1. Specifically defined

2. Measurable

3. Attainable

4. Reasonable

5. Time based

MANY OF YOU will recognise this as the SMART model for goal setting that is often used in business. Let's take the first element: specifically defined. You might say to yourself, 'I want to quit my job', or, 'I want to retire early'. While these are great ideas, they are not specific, so there's no way to measure how close you are to achieving them – or whether you are falling behind, or ahead of where you should be. A better way to phrase this goal might be, 'I want to make X number of dollars so that I can resign from my job at age fifty and retire early'.

Most people respond better to specific goals than to general ones, such as 'do better', or 'be the best'. Specific goals will give you a target to aim for, which will give you some sense of how far you have to go. A good goal will tell you how, when, where, and by what means so that you can track your progress.

Let's take the retirement goal again. If you are going to make, let's say, $2 million and retire by the age of fifty, then you need to list possibilities. They might include buying X number of properties each year. If you don't have much time, it might include choosing properties in areas that have the potential for double-digit appreciation. Get creative with ways to meet your goal.

It is important during this process that you not confuse goals and tasks. Goals are the big targets, and tasks are the small steps that get you there. For example, if your goal is to buy one property every month, then a task might be meeting with your sales agent each week to go over potential properties. Accomplishing small tasks working toward your goal every day is important because it gives you a sense of control and accomplishment. However, be sure that all the small tasks are all working toward the goal. It is easy to seem very busy but, in truth, to not achieve anything. Write down each activity you perform on the path to your goal, and evaluate it on a weekly or monthly basis. This will tell you if you are spending too much time on things that are not moving you forward.

LONG HORIZON AND SHORT HORIZON GOALS

Everyone needs both long- and short-horizon goals. Some short-horizon goals are based on a sense of urgency; for example, 'Clean up my credit in the next six months to be able to borrow the most money possible at a great interest rate'. Others are small steps to reach your long-horizon goals, as in, 'Take all investment profits and reinvest in more properties for at least the next five years'.

So why not just make the big, long-horizon goals and do away with all these short-horizon goals? Humans perform better with regular and consistent reinforcement. As you track your progress and see how many short-horizon goals you have accomplished, it makes the long-horizon goals seem that much more attainable.

Long-horizon goals have an important function as well. In addition to giving you an overall direction, they also provide a focal point when money gets tight or you suffer setbacks. Focusing on the long-horizon goal and being able to see the big picture can get you through those times when it would be easy to quit. It allows you to see your situation as temporary and gives you the will to search for solutions. As you overcome each difficulty, it builds the confidence you will need to push on toward that long-horizon goal.

> *If you have accomplished all that you have planned for*
> *yourself, you have not planned enough.*
> *– Edward Everett Hale (1822 – 1909),*
> *American Minister and Writer*

THE FOLLOWING ARE some examples of how to take each long-horizon goal and break it down into accomplishable, short-horizon goals – and then further break these down into individual tasks.

BUSINESS GOALS

LONG-HORIZON GOAL:

1. Achieve the best interest rates and start accumulating properties at the rate of one or two properties per year.

SHORT-HORIZON GOAL:

2. Reduce any unnecessary debt, especially 'bad debt' (debt that does not create an income or asset, such as personal loans for furniture or cars) over the next six months, and look into creative financing options.

TASKS RELATED TO SHORT-HORIZON GOAL:

1. Frequently check and clean up credit.

2. Pay off credit cards and put money in savings.

3. Start accumulating properties using alternative financing, such as owner financing.

PROCRASTINATION IS NOT your friend when it comes to setting goals. This is why so many people get to the end of the year and realise that the goals they set last year didn't budge an inch. They put off working on them each week, then each month, until a whole year has passed. The world keeps moving forward whether you do or not, and by standing still, you get left behind.

Just the activity of setting goals can be highly motivating, but in order to sustain that motivation, you have to choose goals that are within your realm of control and within a realistic timetable. What does this mean? A good example might be if you decide that you want to make a million dollars and have your own reality TV show in one year. While you may be able to accomplish both of these goals in the long term, the timetable of one year is probably unrealistic. You have to have certain skills to accomplish both of these goals, and they take time to master.

Just as it is unrealistic to think you can lose 5 kg in a month and keep it off, it is also unrealistic to think that you can make a million dollars in a year in real estate and have any idea how to hang on the money or reproduce it consistently. You have to put in the time to learn the business, and it will pay off for you in the end. I'm not saying you can't get lucky and hit a jackpot property, but just don't expect it. If it happens, be grateful.

While it may seem that all of this planning, believing, and thinking about your goals is wasting time you could spend achieving them, it is not. Remember, I said that knowing what not to do is almost as important as knowing what to do. Learning from others, especially from mentors, saves time by allowing you to avoid the pitfalls they have experienced. Every setback you can avoid is time saved toward achieving your long-horizon goal.

Many obstacles can and will get in your way as you strive toward your goals. Focusing on your plan and visualizing where you want to go gives you a clear path and helps you avoid life's challenges.

I'm grateful for all my problems. As each of them was overcome
I became stronger and more able to meet those yet to come.
I grew on my difficulties.
– J.C. Penney (1875 – 1971), American Retailing Magnate

THE OPPOSITE END of the spectrum is setting goals that are too low. Something that is easily attainable barely qualifies as a goal at all. Try not to underestimate yourself or discount the skills you already possess. Often people become easily bored with goals that are too easily met. They lose interest, and you will too.

You must pick goals that challenge you professionally, mentally, and even spiritually. Go for the projects and properties that make you stretch your possibilities and require a high level of creativity to meet. You will never achieve great things without pushing yourself. Goals that don't push you move you sideways rather than forward. They do not move you out of your comfort zone or force you to learn new and difficult things. It takes three key factors to reach any goal: commitment, plan, and action.

SETTING THE GOAL

BEING SERIOUS ABOUT a goal means that you take the necessary steps, whatever those may be, to achieve it. Give yourself self-imposed deadlines for specific tasks and evaluate your own progress in a businesslike and objective manner. You can then develop the next set of strategic tasks and move forward. The first step to becoming serious is to write down your goal. The second step is to announce it publicly. This may seem like you are giving those around you the opportunity to ridicule you in advance – and some may. However, by first writing your goal down, you are starting the power of belief. By announcing it, you then receive additional motivation since you know that people will be asking about your progress. This gives you not only accountability to yourself, but also to others.

You have probably heard people close to you announce their plans, but how did they do it? Did they say, 'I'm going to make $250,000 next year and drive a Mercedes', or did they say something like, 'I'm going to make more money and get a new car'?

COMMITMENT

IF YOU HEARD someone make the first statement, you would assume that they were serious and committed to their goals. However, if you heard the second statement, you would wonder how serious they were, or if this was just a wish or dream of theirs with no possibility of happening. This person, instead of setting a goal and being willing to work hard to achieve it, is content to just wish and get nowhere. Here again, procrastination is not your friend. If you are thinking that you will start working toward you property-investment goals after the holidays, on your birthday, or after a particular event happens, you are just wishing. Every day you waste is a day further away from achieving your goals.

The second key factor to reaching your goal is flexibility. This does not mean making excuses for your lack of progress. This means using all of your talents and creativity to overcome obstacles, while listening to constructive criticism. This will help you clarify your goals as you go. You must have the ability to step back on a regular basis (I recommend at least monthly) and evaluate your progress. What worked? What didn't? What changes are you going to make in your strategy and task list for next month? Remember the saying, 'The definition of insanity is doing the same thing day in and day out and expecting different results'.

PLANNING

REMEMBER THAT I said goal planning involves risk? This means risking a wrong move, bad decision, and even a major setback. It also means that you must be adaptable to changing circumstances. You must still juggle a job, family, and bills in addition to striving toward your investment goals.

There are times when certain goals will take a backseat to others temporarily out of necessity, but all of these instances give you the opportunity to be creative and perhaps even come up with another opportunity that fits into your long-horizon goals.

Feedback is important because no one knows everything. No matter how well you have researched or planned, there may be some areas that you have overlooked or are unaware of. It is also possible that you may also lose your perspective from time to time and be unable to correctly assess your own efforts. At those times, a wise or experienced friend or mentor can help you get back on track.

Friends and advisors who are aware of your desire to invest in property will also be able to offer encouragement. Your friends and mentors can offer feedback and give you a moral boost when you need it. Talk to them about where you are on the path toward your goals, what progress you've made, and what challenges you have encountered. They may be able to offer suggestion or solutions.

We all experience doubts on occasion and suffer through crises of faith in our goals and ourselves. Family and friends who may tell you everything that you can't do, and who discourage you from moving forward can compound these. You must remember to focus on your plan. This means not letting your emotions overwhelm you to the point where you try to prove everyone wrong. While harsh comments may motivate you to strive toward your goal, they may also lead you into self-sabotaging behaviour. If you try to rush and accelerate your plan to prove something, it can lead to disaster.

It is important to guard yourself against this kind of reaction. Stick to your plan and avoid the traps. If you make a mistake, forgive yourself and start again. Build on what you have and learn from each lesson. If you feel in control, and if you are making progress, then it is easier to keep going. You are most certainly your worst critic. Leave your mistakes in the past, however, and continue to move forward.

Your business plan is your roadmap to success. It helps you determine the steps to take to make your real estate investment dreams a reality. Before you go about looking at properties, it is first important to consider what you want to accomplish and how you will get there. Most real estate investors start quite small, with one or two properties, and then build from there. Many still continue to work their regular jobs and manage the properties on the side.

By planning where you eventually want to go, you can make those first steps in the right direction. You may have a dream to accumulate numerous single-family homes and eventually turn the management over to a professional property-management company. Or you may have a dream of owning numerous apartment buildings or even commercial properties. No matter what dream suits you best, you can begin by starting small and working toward that dream.

Doing is better than saying.
– Proverb

BUDGETING

MANY PEOPLE WHO hear my personal story of how I have accumulated properties by cutting back and living on much less still think it is out of reach for them. They and their spouse may work full time, and with children and all their activities, the money seems to flow out almost as quickly as it comes in. The idea of coming up with any amount to invest seems near impossible. However, we often become accustomed to living a particular lifestyle and spending what we earn. How much of your last pay rise have you saved? By simply sitting down and evaluating those expenses that are not really critical, you can begin to free up some money to invest. You will also be surprised how a simple restructuring of certain types of debt can also free up additional money.

The first step is to evaluate where all of your money goes. This entails making a realistic list, which means using actual expenses – not what you think you spend. Get your bank and credit card statements and use actual numbers for the following categories. There may even be some other categories that you need to add to account for what you spend; the following categories are just to get you started.

EXPENSES:

Mortgage/Rent Payments _____

Telephone _____

Television _____

Internet _____

Electricity_____

Gas_____

Water _____

Council Rates _____

Home Maintenance (cleaning, repairs, yard work) _____

Food: Eating out _____

Groceries _____

Clothing _____

Vehicle(s) Loan/Lease Payments _____

Fuel _____

Repairs _____

Insurance _____

Entertainment _____

School Fees _____

Childcare _____

Children's Activities (piano, soccer, etc.) _____

Personal Loans _____

Credit Cards _____

Memberships (clubs, gym, etc.) _____

Gifts/Donations _____

TOTAL MONTHLY EXPENSES: _____

Income: _____

Wages _____

Commission _____

Contract Work _____

Rental Income _____

Shares _____

Other Income _____

TOTAL MONTHLY INCOME: _____

NOW SUBTRACT YOUR expenses from your income. This is the amount you have left over each month. Does it seem realistic, or have you perhaps missed something? Are you disappointed at how small an amount there is? Don't let it get you down! As we've already talked about, we tend to expand our lives in relation to the money coming in so as to take up all available resource each month. It's not unusual to spend what you earn, but you can choose to break that habit and create a new one that will improve your life over the long run. It's also not that uncommon for your outgoing expenses to slightly exceed your income – thus the payment shuffle that many people experience at the end of each month. Don't worry, I'll show you a few quick and easy steps to find more cash that can be used to start your real estate business.

As you look over all the expenses that you currently have, what do you see that can be cut? Many people are quite surprised when they write down exactly what they spend. It is very much like writing down every bite you eat; you will be amazed at how often you spend without even thinking about it. That morning coffee and snack can add up to a bundle, not only on your waistline, but on your budget as well! What about your shopping habits? Have they gotten a bit out of hand? Do you really need everything you have purchased in the last month? What about all those dinners out with friends? Can you have a barbecue with them at home for less money and still enjoy your time socializing?

One of the areas many people struggle with is debt. Getting rid of personal loans and credit cards will save you a bundle each month – and improve your credit scores. It is often helpful to either get a consolidation loan or to pay down the debt with some of your home equity. A word of caution, however: be sure you don't slide back into the habits that created the debt in the first place, and pay the consolidation loan off as quickly as possible.

Many people find that at least 10 to 15 per cent of expenses can be cut, and often more. Once you eliminate some expenses, then it's time to look at your income. Can you work additional hours at your job? What about a second job? Although the Australian tax office will tax you at a higher rate for having two jobs, sometimes it can be worth it if it allows you to buy assets that produce a stream of income or that appreciate as quickly as property does.

If you are struggling with trying to create a budget, there are several good software packages that can help. David Wright has designed a program called Simply Budgets that can have amazing results for your life and savings plan. You can also read books on home budgeting and credit repair that can give many more tips and strategies than I offer here. No matter what path you choose, the important part is to seriously look at all your options and find a way to make your dream happen.

A MOVING TARGET

WHEN YOU THINK about the amount of money or assets that you will need to become financially independent, it can be difficult to guess what that dollar amount may be. Since prices and wages escalate every single year, the money you earn this year will be worth less and buy less next year. You must also take into account the lifestyle that you wish to maintain and the rate of interest that your investments earn. While one million dollars may sound like a lot to you right now, twenty years down the road, I guarantee that it will not. There are numerous free financial calculators on the Internet that can help you figure out the amount you will need. The following are a few specific examples, but you can locate a retirement calculator and find the right number for you.

DWAINE INVESTS IN SHARES

He is forty-five years old and earns $50,000. He is currently putting $5000 per year (10 per cent) into his share account, which now totals $100,000 and earns an average of 10 per cent over time. He wants to retire in twenty years, and his goal is to live at least as well as he is right now. Sounds like a sound plan, doesn't it? Here is what Dwaine will be looking at:

By age sixty-five, Dwaine will have amassed $945,679* – almost a million dollars! But wait. It will now cost him significantly more to live. This will eat up the interest he is earning plus the principal, and by age seventy-four, Dwaine will be completely out of money! So much for that million dollars. This example also assumes that the market doesn't take a tumble right before he retires, which could make much of his savings evaporate.

*Assuming 4 per cent inflation and 4 per cent annual pay increases. I've also assumed that he will choose safer investments when he retires and earn 5 per cent on his account. These calculations were made using the tools at www.bloomberg.com.

WITH THIS EXAMPLE, it becomes clear that Dwaine needs much more than one million dollars just to maintain his current lifestyle in retirement. On his income, how will he ever be able to do it? The answer is property.

Think back to the example of Adam, who used $150,000 to buy four properties at $300,000 each:

ADAM'S PORTFOLIO

Year	Rate PA	Four Properties at $300,000 each	Total Increase PA
Start	8%	1,200,000.00	Nil
1	8%	1,296,000.00	96,000.00
2	8%	1,399,680.00	103,680.00
3	8%	1,511,654.40	111,974.40
4	8%	1,632,586.75	120,932.35
5	8%	1,763,193.69	130,606.94
6	8%	1,904,249.19	141,055.50
7	8%	2,056,589.12	152,339.94
8	8%	2,221,116.25	164,527.13
9	8%	2,398,805.55	177,689.30
10	8%	2,590,710.00	191,904.44
Value			
Less Initial Cost		1,200,000.00	
Total Capital Gain		$1,390,710.00	

IF ADAM WERE to take this capital gain and pay a maximum of 50 per cent capital gain tax and reinvested the balance in exactly this same manner for the next ten years, he will amass $6,445,940! And that is not even including any gain in the assets after he retires. His money will also not be subject to the volatility of the open market, as real estate has historically always gone up. Adam will be able to retire early and live very well due to his investment in property.

CHAPTER 6
MY BUSINESS PLAN

1.   Investigate the various business structures and decide which is best for you.

2.   Taxes are one of the main concerns when choosing a business structure.

3.   Don't overlook insurance when creating your business plan.

4.   Devote a specific time schedule to your real estate investing and portfolio.

5.   Write down your business goals.

6.   Set long- and short-horizon goals.

7.   Look at your income and expenses, and determine how you can cut back to invest more.

8.   Make a budget and stick to it in order to reach your goals.

MY ACTION PLAN AND NOTES

_____

_____

_____

_____

_____

_____

_____

_____

_____

_____

_____

CHAPTER

7

MY RESEARCH:

DUE DILIGENCE IS THE KEY TO

BUYING THE PERFECT PROPERTY

CHAPTER 7

MY RESEARCH:
DUE DILIGENCE IS THE KEY TO
BUYING THE PERFECT PROPERTY

When you know what you want, and you want it bad enough,
you will find a way to get it.
– Jim Rohn, Business Philosopher

Research is an important part of being a property investor. Though you may be tempted to skip certain aspects of researching a particular area on occasion, you will never regret sticking to your program and uncovering each bit of valuable information that could make or break your next real estate deal.

I knew clients who sourced a property in a booming mining area. They subsequently purchased it. Previous years showed growth of 30–40 per cent per annum. The challenge was that there was only one industry in the area responsible for the booming economy. The issue these clients faced was that when the industry slowed down, so did the new employment and new residents to the area. In turn, many investors were left without tenants and had difficulty selling their properties, as no one was moving to the area or wanting to buy.

If these clients had conducted their research with more diligence, they would have found that if there is only one industry supporting the economy in an area, there is higher risk. If the industry slows down or closes up, what do the locals do? They move to another area where there is work. There are numerous areas around Australia where this happens even today. Be very aware of covering all your bases when investigating areas that are new to you.

It is important to know which aspects of your local property market are the most important to research, and how this translates into financial potential. We will also talk about how to recognise what you are looking for when you drive up to a property for the first time. What are the potential details that could indicate a dud in disguise? What do you want to avoid?

Asking the following questions will give answers to the basic guideline I recommend when seeking the right area and property for you:

1. Do you want capital growth or rental yield?

2. Should you buy in your own area?

3. What type of tenants do you want to attract? What are the demographics of the area?

4. What is happening with the infrastructure, development, and town planning?

5. What types of industry and business support the economy? Is the population growing due to employment?

6. Can you increase the value of the property easily?

7. Where is the area on the property cycle?

8. Where can you find the information you need to evaluate the property?

CAPITAL GROWTH OR RENTAL YIELD

FIRST, YOU MUST decide whether capital growth or rental yield is more important to you. If you decide on capital growth, it usually means the property will be negative geared, which will create a larger tax deduction each year. A property is called negative geared if the expenses are higher than the income for the year, therefore making the property a tax deduction against your full income for the year. If you decide you want to receive higher rental yield or income, it generally means you will see lower growth in the coming years. I am personally a fan of capital growth, as it enables me to leverage into further properties each year with the growth in equity from existing properties. Keep in mind that to continually purchase high-growth properties, you will need good cash flow from other sources of income to help substantiate the mortgage interests while the rental income catches up. I believe that both types of properties have their place in an investor's portfolio, as it diversifies their investments. I would suggest that you speak to your accountant to be sure what is best for your circumstances.

BUYING IN YOUR AREA

YOU'VE PROBABLY OFTEN heard property investment people talk about the virtues of location, location, location, and it's true. The location of a piece of property is one thing that can't be changed, so it is important to get it right. When you are first starting as an investor, I usually recommend that you buy something close to where you live now, or in an area that you know well. Since you may manage some aspects of the property, such as maintenance, there's no use in driving a long distance for a leaky tap. It is also great to purchase your first property in an area that you know well because you will not need to conduct as much research. There will be things you already know about the area, such as what the council has planned, and the main industry and business of the area. Be sure you purchase this property based on the numbers and facts and not the emotions you may feel about an area.

Once you have chosen a good area, close to where you live, you will want to look at that area very closely. There are several factors that will determine which particular neighbourhoods should be considered.

We talked earlier in the book about owner-occupied properties, and how a high percentage of these in a given neighbourhood made the rental more valuable. Many people refer to this as pride of ownership. If you take a short drive through a neighbourhood you are considering, notice whether many have yards that are neat and tidy. Do the homes look well maintained? Are any vacant lots free of clutter and well kept? Nobody wants to live in an area that is in a declining condition, with old cars sitting on the lawn and graffiti everywhere. They want community – a place that looks like home. This is why if you get a good price on a house located in a great area of town that needs a little work, you should seriously consider it, since you know the long-term prospects for this property can be good and you can add immediate value with a renovation.

Look in the immediate vicinity for major employers. The cost of commuting is skyrocketing for most people, so it has become a big factor in considering their housing options. The same is true for retailers. People like to shop close to home, so take note of how close the area is to good shopping areas and restaurants. If retailers are moving to another area of town and there are vacant shops, you might want to reconsider.

Access to things such as major roads, hospitals, utilities, fire stations, and emergency access are also important. Are the roads well maintained? Are there any new construction projects or highways planned that will effect property values? Are the local hospitals, fire stations, and ambulance services readily available and responsive? What utilities are available, and what, if any, new private developments or council projects are planned? Does the area recycle and have rubbish removal? All of this inquiry will give you an idea of not only they type of property to buy, but also what the offer should be for the property you have in mind.

Once you become experienced, you may wish to look elsewhere, especially if your area has a lack of growth potential. You could start with a town of at least 30,000-50,000 people in order to have enough demand for your rental property. This doesn't mean that you absolutely can't invest in a smaller town, but it exposes you to the possibility that your property may stay vacant for long periods.

TYPE OF TENANTS OR DEMOGRAPHICS

DEMOGRAPHICS ARE ALSO very important. This is the breakdown of what types of people live in a particular area. Understanding the demographics will allow you to see if the renters you want for a particular property exist in large enough numbers for it to stay consistently rented. A demographic survey will also help you determine if another type of rental property might be more in line with the population. For example, if there are a large number of retirees, then homes for large families are not going to be the prime rental base. You might need to look at units, as many people tend to downsize when they retire.

Rental managers in the area can give you information on how long a typical property stays vacant, and what the rental increases have been over the past few years. This is also a good time to ask questions of the managers. Find out how many properties they manage and what their experience has been in the area. These managers are well versed in the local rental market and can offer excellent opinions. When you ask about vacancy rates, you should not consider an area where the rates are above 5 per cent. The lower the better.

You cannot succeed by yourself. It is hard to find a rich hermit.
– Jim Rohn, Business Philosopher

COUNCIL PLANS, INFRASTRUCTURE, AND DEVELOPMENT

YOU MAY ALSO take a trip to the council and see what there is to see and do in your location. Things such as a lot of nearby shops, restaurants, universities, and so forth will entice people to be more willing to live in the area, and consequently, you will have lower vacancy rates.

The area and neighbourhoods around universities are also great places to acquire small rental properties. The homes surrounding these schools are usually well kept, and many of the students and professionals who work at the university look for housing close by, so investigate these opportunities as well.

If you don't have school-age children, then you may think that the quality of the local schools is not a big concern – but it should be. If you are trying to rent a family home, schools and their ranking in the community are a determining factor for many people when they choose where to live. Most will pay more for housing in an area with excellent schools, and renters with children will stay longer in a property than those who do not have children. Most schools have their own website now where their scores and student results are listed. You may also want to talk to a local property manger familiar with the area who can quickly tell you which areas are the most in demand for families with school-age children.

INDUSTRY, BUSINESS, AND POPULATION GROWTH

OTHER STATISTICS TO look at are population and growth. You should choose an area that shows a net gain in population over the past few years. This will ensure that people are not abandoning the area for somewhere better. Along the same lines, it is good to step back and look at the regional economy. Assess if it is improving and its rate of growth. Who are the major employers, and are they stable? What kinds of jobs are they providing? Are they high-paying, professional positions, or middle-income positions?

ADDING VALUE TO PROPERTIES

MANY INVESTORS START their business by purchasing renovators. They refurbish these properties and use them as rental properties. This allows them to have a greater gain in equity faster than if they bought one that needed no work. It also allows them to immediately take out a loan for more money than they would be able to normally.

If this is your plan, then you will be able to find numerous opportunities in almost any area, but you must be knowledgeable and understand what you are looking for when you review a property. This is a good time to bring along your mentor who can point out opportunities for greater gain and help steer you away from possible disasters.

When looking for a refurbish/rental that will offer a substantial gain, remember that location is still extremely important. The goal with these types of properties is to acquire the biggest net increase in value. When looking for renovators in the better neighbourhoods, consider the phrase, 'Worst house on the best street'. With this type of purchase, you have a much higher chance of netting a sizable gain. If you try to buy distressed property in a declining area of town, you run the risk of putting more into the property that it will be worth in the following years, which is referred to as over-capitalising.

Look for properties that need cosmetic work only. Cosmetic work means that the properties are structurally sound and have good plumbing and electrical systems. If you spend a relatively small amount of money, then many of these properties can see tremendous gains in value.

Renovators are also a great property to start with, as they are generally low in price – in fact, quite often underpriced – due to their condition. This is especially true of homes where the garden is so overgrown you can barely see the house. These properties can be little gems. How wonderful would it be to buy a property for $80,000 less than the others on the same street, and then spend a few weeks renovating it, at a cost to you of only $15,000? What if, after those two weeks, you had the property revalued, and it was already worth $100,000 more than you paid for it? It would be a pretty good return for a few weeks' effort!

Profits are better than wages. Wages made you a living;
profits make you a fortune.
– Jim Rohn, Business Philosopher

AS I MENTIONED, look for properties that need minor work, unless, of course, you are quite handy. I have had clients over the years who took the time to do the minor repairs that only required a week or two of work and a bit of elbow grease, and the results were amazing. Renovations that I recommend to improve sales value and also rental yield are:

PAINTING

PAINT HAS THE amazing ability to make an old room look new. It hides all the sins of previous occupiers for very little cost. I highly recommend that you patch any plaster damage and remove all hooks and nails before painting. If you are going to the effort to paint a wall, you should prepare it well. It's easy to tell whether it was painted as a quickie job, which will affect the amount that future buyers will pay and the quality of the future renters of the property. A must for paint selection is neutral shades such as off whites and pale cream colours. Trends and fashions change, and your property should appeal to the widest range of future occupiers and match their personal belongings. Keep it plain and simple.

FLOORING

FLOORS ARE ONE element of a home that show extreme wear. It is great having newly painted walls, but if the floor is in terrible condition, the paintwork will mock the floors. Carpets are relatively cheap and simple to replace. Frequently, if the existing carpet is stretched and rippling, it is easier and more cost effective to have a carpet layer re-stretch it to improve the appearance than it is to replace the carpet. A better option yet – if the property has a timber floor – is to pull up the floor coverings and polish the boards. This can literally change the whole appearance of the room, and it looks amazing if done well.

Personally, I think all rental properties should have hard floors, as one of the most common challenges landlords encounter is damaged floor coverings – and it is very difficult to reinstate them or to force tenants to replace them. One of my properties on the Gold Coast, I would have to say, is the most perfect rental property. It has timber floors throughout, a basic Laminex kitchen and bathroom, and neatly painted, neutral walls. One tenant leaves without the expense of carpet cleaning, and the next one moves in. Parents particularly love timber floors or any hard floor, as they can mop the floor and keep it clean for their families.

KITCHENS

THIS IS AN area that can blow out the cost if you are not careful. Look inside the cupboards. Sometimes you can use the existing framework and just replace the cupboard fronts and bench tops. Or better still, you may be able to use the same bench top if you just Laminex the top.

One of my own properties that I renovated had an original, old, timber-frame kitchen, but the framework and shelving were in perfect condition. My highly talented builder at the time suggested we use dowel rods to frame a square on the front of the doors, and then paint them. We also put on the solid timber bench top, and the end result was beautiful. Friends and family who would visit loved it. If only they knew how simple and cost effect the renovation was!

We now have ability to paint tiles. Old tiles can be very gaudy in colour, and as with wall colours and floors tiles, they are best suited to neutral tones because the average person tends to go for neutral, simple tones and colours.

BATHROOMS

THIS, TOO, CAN be an area of hidden cost. Replacing vanities is cost effective if you stick to a standard, pre-made cupboard, sink, and tap fixtures. If the shower is tiled, check for any evidence of leaks. There are sealing products available that you can apply to the grout to prevent leaks. Shower screens are an easy replacement also. Baths can be resealed, but always get a quote first and make sure that it wouldn't be cheaper in the long run to replace it with a new one.

FIXTURES AND FITTINGS

CURTAINS, BLINDS, OR other window coverings can be cleaned and refitted. There are also plenty of options to purchase pre-made blinds that modernise any room. Pre-made curtains can be fitted immediately, and if they are too long, you simply increase the hem. Light fittings and power points can make a great overall finishing touch if replaced. Hunt around and you will find some bargains for window covers and light fittings.

HOUSE EXTERIOR

PAINTING CAN CHANGE the complete look of a house. It can make the most neglected house look loved. Gutters should be cleaned out and painted if needed, along with the eaves. Look for any cracked roof tiles, as these can be replaced individually as required.

LANDSCAPING

THIS IS ONE of the most important areas of the property, as your front garden gives you the first impression and street appeal. Trim the trees, weed the gardens, mow the lawns, and replace any bare spots with instant turf or lawn seed. Mulching the garden can make a huge improvement. This makes the overall appearance look neat and even and gives uniformity to the garden. Check out local markets, as you can buy plants quite cheaply when you purchase them directly from the growers.

Showing a profit means touching something and leaving it
better than you found it.
— Jim Rohn, Business Philosopher

BEWARE THE PIT

A NOTE OF caution – be certain of what a property needs and know how to tell the difference between a small challenge and a money pit. This is a good reason to bring an experienced property renovating professional with you when you look at properties. Some big issues are visible to even the uninitiated, but some are not. Never assume that things are fine.

Don't hesitate to call in the troops. When looking at what you think might be a good buy, it often helps to have a contractor take a look. He or she may have a completely different opinion and can give you a realistic idea of the cost of repairs. The contractor may also suggest ways to cut costs, and can help you develop a budget if the property looks promising. Sticking to a budget is paramount when renovating a house. It is important to remember that you are not building a dream home – you are improving an investment. That's it. It may not make good sense to add some of the more costly amenities, as they don't always add value. Listen to your experts and try to do what will bring the most value for your money.

One strategy that many renovators use is called delayed settlement with a renovation access clause. The purpose of this is to allow an investor to purchase a property from a seller with a longer than usual settlement, and to allow the buyer access to renovate the property prior to settlement. This enables the buyer to work on the property without paying any holding costs. When settlement is reached, the property is completely finished and ready for either renting or selling. Be warned that there is an element of risk to this, as officially the property does not belong to the buyer until settlement. This means that there is a risk of losing the money spent on the property if, for any reason, settlement does not occur.

Here's an example of a delayed settlement with a renovation access clause. Let's say Natalie and Mark find a property to refurbish that is on the market for $250,000. They negotiate a delayed settlement of sixty to ninety days, which allows them access to complete the renovation. The renovations cost $30,000. They then obtain an independent valuation. The increase in value from their additions brings the new valuation to $340,000. This is an increase of $90,000 on the purchase price, or $60,000 after renovation expenses. Natalie and Mark can then use this increase in value by increasing their mortgage, and by purchasing another one or two properties with this money as a deposit.

THE PROPERTY CYCLE

AS IT IS well known, properties go through a cycle. There are approximately four stages in this cycle, and they include:

BOOM

UP TURN

DOWN TURN

STEADY/FLAT

UP TURN

THIS IS WHEN the market is showing signs of growth and, initially, there will be small growth until the market gains momentum. This is a wonderful time to buy; it will be the start of the market changing into a seller's market.

BOOM

THIS IS WHEN property values literally increase weekly or monthly, depending on the area. Unless you purchase at the start of the boom, I would suggest you steer clear of buying in this time, as you can never know for sure when the boom will finish.

DOWN TURN

DOWN TURN IS after the boom period. During this time, many property owners must adapt to the realization that their property is, for example, not realistically worth $500,000 but now, with the downturn, only valued at $470,000. This is the market adjustment time, and it is necessary in all markets. It is also the time that many property owners become distressed, as they may have increased their mortgage in the boom time and are now struggling to meet all their financial commitments. Properties can be bought during this period at a lower rate. But be careful, as you must be sure that the market is not going to decrease further or you may end up in the same situation as some current property owners.

STEADY/FLAT

THIS IS WHEN you will hear many real estate agents call the market 'flat'. Not a lot happens during this time, as the properties are already adjusted to realistic prices. This can also be a good time to buy, as there may be properties on the market that are not moving (although this may mean they are overpriced).

WHERE TO FIND INFORMATION

SPEAK TO THE local council to obtain information about the future town planning, which will provide you with details regarding road upgrades, shopping development plans, and areas they forecast for potential residential development. If you check with the planning department, you can actually see where and for what developers are seeking approval.

Read the local newspaper. This is a valuable source of what is happening in the area, such as business information, local developments, new plans for the area, and what companies are planning to open businesses in the area.

An investment in knowledge always pays the best interest.
– Benjamin Franklin (1706 – 90),
American Statesman and Philosopher

SUBSCRIBE TO REAL estate publications such as Australian Property Investor. I am a huge believer in self-education; you can never know or read too much. You know the saying that a reader is usually more intelligent than a non-reader? If you don't learn something new every day of your life, then what are you doing? You must move forward, otherwise you will go backward.

Real estate Internet sites with area profiles are a brilliant source of information. Most of these sites, like http://www.realestate.com.au, can also provide you with recent sales information. They provide a perfect research tool for rental values and demand.

I also like going to an area and walking around the shopping district. This helps me get a feel for the place. If I have the opportunity to visit the area I am researching, I will make an effort to talk to some locals. Local residents are an invaluable source of information regarding what is happening in their community and which areas are good or bad to live in. They will know what the locals are looking for in rental accommodations.

The Australian Bureau of Statistics (www.abs.gov.au) will help provide information like population growth and demographics, including the age of people in the area and the types of households (single, family, and so forth).

Sales and data history will tell you what you should pay for property in the specific area you are considering. This data tracks recent home sales and can be provided by any local sales agent. It will also tell you the median price for homes selling in the area. A good rule of thumb for getting a good rental property is to choose a home that is right around the median price. This means it is affordable for the majority of the population, and there should be plenty of renters.

Capital growth statistics can give you an idea about the potential appreciation of the property. While you must understand that past performance does not guarantee the amount of capital growth, if you go back and look at the growth over a five, ten, or twelve year period, it can give you a reasonable estimation of the potential.

There is endless information available to us these days with the Internet at our fingertips. I would highly recommend checking out the relevant state website for the Real Estate Institutes around Australia. These websites generally have statistics about high performing areas, state relevant tenancy legislation links, and other industry links that can benefit you.

The sites for each state are as follows:

Australia	REIA	www.reiaustralia.com.au
Australian Capital Territory	RIACT	www.reiact.com.au
Queensland	REIQ	www.reiq.com.au
Victoria	REIV	www.reiv.com.au
New South Wales	REINSW	www.reinsw.com.au

Northern Territory	REINT	www.reint.com.au
South Australia	REISA	www.reisa.com.au
Tasmania	REIT	www.reit.com.au
Western Australia	REIWA	www.reiwa.com.au

OTHER OPPORTUNITIES

MONEY CAN BE MADE in every segment of the property market, and though most of this book has focused on houses, it is not meant to deter you from other areas of the market. Some of the areas that investors like to explore include apartments, student housing, flats, and even holiday apartments. These properties have good and bad attributes, and as long as the investor goes in knowledgably, there is still money to be made.

Often these types of properties are known collectively as low-demand properties. This means that they are very specific and only appeal to one group of individuals in the marketplace. While that can be good if there are many renters in that group, it can also become a liability down the road. Since only one type of renter is interested in that particular type of property, only one type of buyer will be interested when it comes time to sell. This is reflected in the inability of these properties to get the kind of capital growth that other properties enjoy.

Another issue with low demand properties is that they are notoriously hard to finance. Banks will often require a larger deposit, sometimes as much as 40 per cent. This is a reflection of their assessment of risk. For example, they may be less than 40 square metres in size, and therefore are classed as hotel accommodations. Banks know that over time, that particular kind of buyer could become scarce, and the property might not sell as quickly as others – or at all.

High-rise or apartment buildings have their own issues as well. In these instances, property values can fail to grow, or may even fall. If a buyer purchases an off-the-plan apartment, which is an apartment that is due to be built in the future, and selects the apartment they want by looking at the builder's blueprints and buys it prior to it being built with the hope that it will gain appreciation in a couple of years, they could be sorely disappointed. In fact, the value could plummet. Properties such as these are much more susceptible to market swings and fluctuations. Many apartment blocks also have high body corporate fees, which are the levies that each apartment owner contributes to pay ongoing maintenance to the apartment block, like gardening and lawn maintenance. Also, rent can fluctuate depending on the number of apartments in the building. You may have little control over renovations as well.

Having thoroughly frightened you now, I should tell you that these types of specialised properties also have some good points. They can be inexpensive, which works well for people on a lower property budget. Some of them can be spectacularly placed on the waterfront or near beautiful scenery. Pick a corner or large unit, if possible, and look for one with special amenities. Anything you can do to add value to that particular unit over others in the building is advantageous. More and more developers of apartment blocks are looking for facilities that make their development more appealing than the development down the street. Facilities that can increase the value of an apartment block or achieve higher rental income include gyms and saunas, swimming pools, round-the-clock reception, concierge/cleaning services, theatres, onsite libraries, and locations close to cafes and restaurants. With our increasingly busy lifestyles, apartment living in the right location will remain popular with all age groups.

The main concern is that you know what you are doing when you invest in these types of low demand properties. Low demand properties are called this because there is usually only a small group of people that these properties will suit. For example, not everyone will want to rent or buy a one-bedroom apartment or unit because it will only house a single person or a couple. If you study the area you are buying in and find that 70 per cent of households have children, which therefore requires two- to three-bedroom dwellings, then a one-bedroom unit will be classed as a low demand property. Even if you do everything right in avoiding low demand properties, conditions could change in the marketplace, leaving you with no renters and no buyers for the property.

It's important not to leave homes completely out of this category. You can run into a similar scenario by buying a rental home in a poor or high-risk area. The odds of you ever turning a decent profit here are slim.

HOT SPOTS

I KNOW THAT researching can make you feel like the whole process of property selection is too hard, and you may even feel like giving up on this time-consuming activity. But there is help out there. There are a number of companies and individuals whose whole business is researching the next up-and-coming areas to boom. I personally cherish these types of businesses, as they certainly decrease the time I spend on the Internet and phone doing all my own research. I am not saying that you should stop doing any of your own research, but they can definitely save you plenty of effort. If I hear about areas that are forecasted to boom in the coming months or year, I look into them with my own research. You must remember that most of these businesses are based on people's opinion, their statistical research of past results of that area, and the typical property cycle – plus much more.

One of the biggest influences on what makes an area 'hot' is the supply and demand of housing in the area, which is certainly a major consideration in price growth. But I caution you to also look at the long-term sustainability. What happens if the demand slows down? Are there other factors that will still increase the market value of the properties?

We are not creatures of circumstance;
we are creators of circumstance.
– Benjamin Disraeli (1804 – 81),
Former British Prime Minister

IF YOU RECEIVE tips on the next hot spot, I suggest you check for yourself why it is being recommended. The following are some tips that will help you confirm that an area may truly be the next hot spot:

1. Supply and demand.

2. An area with an appealing lifestyle that has consistent population growth.

3. Infrastructure such as proximity to cafes, shopping centres, and popular outdoor activities.

4. Coastal areas, as we are all drawn to the beach and water, seem to be a major growth factor for properties.

5. Holiday destinations are appealing, as they will bring in tourism, which in turn brings in money and growth.

6. Affordability – if the values of properties are still within easy range, this may be a good area to research further. But if they are out of the reach of most people, or if the average property is selling at or over the asking price, this area might already be in the boom cycle. You then need to ask yourself how long the boom will continue if it has already started.

IF YOUR HOT spot is characterised by some or all of the above, chances are the hot-spot forecaster may have found a winner for you. Happy hunting!

CHAPTER 7
MY RESEARCH

1. You will never regret investigating a property thoroughly.

2. Decide if capital growth or rental income is more important to you.

3. Look at buying close to where you live first.

4. Understand the demographics of a particular area before you buy.

5. If you plan to refurbish properties, look for those that need cosmetic work only.

6. Don't hesitate to call in an experienced renovator or contractor to investigate a property.

7. Properties go through cycles. Know what cycle the current market is in before you buy.

8. All types of properties present opportunities as long as you do your research first.

MY ACTION PLAN AND NOTES

CHAPTER
8

MY PROPERTY:
NOW THAT I HAVE FOUND MY
PROPERTY, WHAT DO I DO NEXT?

CHAPTER 8

MY PROPERTY:
NOW THAT I HAVE FOUND MY
PROPERTY, WHAT DO I DO NEXT?

Goals in writing are dreams with deadlines.
– Brian Tracy, Business Philosopher

A fter all the time you have spent researching the area where you want to buy your investment property, it is now time to assess each property based upon its merits. When you start to inspect properties, you will find that you can become easily confused about which property had which facilities, due to the number of properties you will inspect.

Quite often, I point specific features out to clients, especially when a couple is purchasing the property and only one person is able to inspect it. I will point out colour schemes and the property's features, as I often get phone calls after the inspection with questions like, 'What was the colour of the walls, carpet, or curtains?' These features are some of the first to be forgotten.

It is helpful to work from a checklist to help you remember which property had which features. The following chart is an example, but you can make you own, depending on the particular features and aspects that you feel are important.

The Property Assessment Checklist
Source of Property
Agency Details
Agent Contact / Phone
Property Address
Asking Price
Terms *Vacant Possession / Tenanted*
Facing Aspect *North / South / East / West*
Personal Comments
Type of Property *e.g.: House, Unit, Apartment, Renovator*
Construction *e.g.: Brick Veneer / Weatherboard*
Roof *e.g.: Tiles / Iron*
Interior Lining *e.g.: Plasterboard / Fibro*
Number of Bedrooms *BIR / WIR*
Number of Living Areas
Number of Bathrooms *Bath 1 – Shower, Toilet, Bath, Bath 2 – Shower, Toilet, Bath*
Vehicle Accommodations *e.g.: Double Garage / Carport*
Utilities *e.g.: Gas / Electric / Broadband / Cable TV*
Internal Facilities *Dishwasher, Air Conditioning, Hot Plates / Stove, Range Hood, Spa bath, Security Screens, Alarm System*
External Facilities *Garden Shed, Garden Lights, Water System, Rain Water Tank, BBQ*
Fit Out *Carpets, Tiles, Floorboards, Vinyl, Cork, Floating Boards*
Comments on Standard of Fit Out
General Condition Comments

IT IS ALSO a good idea to write some basic income and expense information relating to each property. You can use a simple table, such as the following, to keep this record.

PROPERTY ADDRESS _____

INCOME	
Rented / Current Amount	$
Can the Rent be Increased? Yes / No Amount	$
Vacant / What Is the Market Rent?	$
TOTAL	$

EXPENSES	
Council Rates	$
Body Corporate	$
Other Expenses	$
TOTAL	$

ONCE YOU START reading property advertisements on the Internet and in newspapers, you'll see that agents often abbreviate real estate terms to reduce advertisement sizes and costs. The following is a list of common abbreviations that may help you interpret the ads:

ac	air conditioning
bi	built in
bir	built-in-robe
br	bedroom
cnr	corner
crpt	carpet
cpds	cupboards
dep	deposit
det	detached
din rm	dining room
dble	double
dbr	double bedroom
elf	electric light fittings
encl	enclosed
estab	established
ext	external
fib	fibro cement
fitts	fittings
fl covs	floor coverings
f/furn	fully furnished
f tld	fully tiled
gi	galvanised iron
grge	garage
htr	heater
hws	hot water service
ig pl	in-ground pool
int	interest
intl	internal
kit	kitchen
k'ette	kitchenette
lge	large
l/fitt	light fittings
liv	living
lnge	lounge
lug	lock-up garage
mstr	master

mtge	mortgage
oil/htr	oil heater
ofp	open fireplace
ono	or nearest offer
oyo	own your own
osp	off-street parking
ped bsn	pedestal basin
pa	per annum
pm	per month
pw	per week
pol flr	polished floor
qual	quality
rec	recess
ren	renovated
rend	rendered
rc	reverse cycle
rm	room
sc	self-contained
s'out	sleep out
spac	spacious
tld rf	tiled roof
tmbr	timber
vp	vacant possession
wc	water closet
wir	walk-in robe
wb	weatherboard
wi	wrought iron

WHEN NEGOTIATING THE purchase of the property, it is important that you find out what fixtures and fittings are included in the sale. Sometimes if a tenant is currently renting the property you purchase, and if the salesperson is not up to date with what belongs to the tenant and what belongs to the owner, there can be assumptions made as to the inclusions. An example could be if the tenant has installed an air conditioning unit into the window, or has a dishwasher fitted into the allocated dishwasher space.

Fixtures and fittings can be included in sales contracts. The following is a list of possible inclusions that can come with a property.

INTERNAL

Dishwasher	Ceiling Fans	Floor Coverings
Furniture	Heaters	Air Conditioners
Curtains and Blinds	Stove	Clothes Dryer
Dryer	Water Filter	Refrigerators
Alarm System	Light Fittings	Freestanding Cupboards
Freestanding Pantry	Remote Controls	Bar
Freestanding Wardrobe		

EXTERNAL

Garden Shed	Fly Screens	Garden Furniture
Barbecue and Gas Bottles	Awnings and Sails	Hot House
TV Aerial	Clothes Line	Watering System
Satellite Dish	Garden Ornaments	Swimming Pool Accessories
Garden Lights		

EXPENSES AND INCOME

There are numerous expenses related to acquiring and owning a rental property. Some of these are one-time expenses, while others are ongoing. It is important to know the difference when calculating your actual return on investment.

ONE-TIME COSTS

ACQUIRING COSTS
- Initial deposit
- Improvements
- Building and termite inspection
- Buyer's agent commission (if applicable)

SETTLEMENT COSTS
- Solicitor's conveyancing fees
- Stamp duty
- Council rates and water rates adjustments

LOAN COSTS
- Establishment fees
- Mortgage stamp duty (see formula for each state's duty on the following pages)
- Mortgage insurance
- Lender's legal fees
- Valuation fees
- Mortgage registration
- Title registration

INVESTMENT SET-UP COSTS
- Depreciation schedule

CREATE A TABLE and fill in all of the fees to give you a true picture of the costs. The following is an example of a property purchase of $250,000. (Note: Costs, government duties, financial dues, and legal fees are example amounts only.)

COST DETAILS
WHEN PAYABLE PERIOD

	UPON SIGNING	CONTRACT	AT SETTLEMENT
Deposit	12,500.00		
Building/Termite		400.00	
Depreciation Report			350.00
Buyer's Agent			6,875.00
Conveyancing Fees			1,000.00
Stamp Duty			12,000.00
Loan Establishment			600.00
Mortgage Insurance			2,800.00
Other Finance Fees			12,000.00
Council Adjustments			150.00
Balance of Purchase			237,500.00
SUB TOTALS	12,500.00	400.00	273,275.00
GRAND TOTAL			**$286,175.00**

FOLLOWING IS A list of the State Stamp Duty Formulas for each state. Some states have different stamp duty amounts for owner-occupied properties (a property you buy to live in) and investment properties. There is also the consideration of reduced levies, depending on individual circumstances, but this generally relates to first-time home buyers or lower-income buyers purchasing a property to live in. These formulas are a guide only, and I recommend that you check with the State Government Treasury or Office of State Revenue in the relevant state, as these formulas can change with legislation amendments.

QUEENSLAND

$20,000	1.5% of assessable or purchase amount
$20,001–$50,000	$300 + 2.25% over $20,001
$50,001–$100,000	$975 + 2.75% over $50,001
$100,001–$250,000	$2350 + 3.25% over $100,001
$250,001–$500,000	$7225 + 3.5% over $250,001
$500,000	$15,975 + 3.75% over $500,001

VICTORIA

$20,000	1.4% of assessable or purchase amount
$20,001–$115,000	$280 + 2.4% over $20,001
$115,001–$870,000	$2,560 + 6% over $115,001
$870,000	5.5% of assessable or purchase amount

SOUTH AUSTRALIA

$12,000	1% of assessable or purchase amount
$12,001–$30,000	$120 + 2% over $12,001
$50,001–$100,000	$1080 + 3.5% over $50,001
$100,001–$200,000	$2830 + 4% over $100,001
$200,001–$250,000	$6830 + 4.25% over $200,001
$250,001–$300,000	$8955 + 4.75% over $250,001
$300,001–$500,000	$11,330 + 5% over $300,001
$500,001	$21,330 + 5.5% over $500,001

NEW SOUTH WALES

$14,000	1.25% of assessable or purchase amount
$14,001–$30,000	$175 + 1.5% over $14,001
$30,001–$80,000	$415 + 1.75% over $30,001
$80,001–$300,000	$1,290 + 3.5% over $80,001
$300,001–$1 million	$8,990 + 4.5% over $300,001
$1 million	$40,490 + 5.5% over 1 million

WESTERN AUSTRALIA

$80,000	2% of assessable or purchase amount
$80,001–$100,000	$1600 + 3% over $80,001
$100,001–$250,000	$2200 + 4% over $100,001
$250,001–$500,000	$8200 + 5% over $250,001
$500,000	$20,700 + 5.4% over $500,000

TASMANIA

$1300	$20
$1,301–$10,0001	5% of assessable or purchase amount
$10,001–$30,000	$150 + 2% over $10,001
$30,001–$75,000	$550 + 2.5% over $30,001
$75,001–$150,000	$1675 + 3% over $75,001
$150,001–$225,000	$3925 + 3.5% over $150,001
$225,001	$6,550 + 4% over $225,001

AUSTRALIAN CAPITAL TERRITORY

$100,000	2% of assessable or purchase amount
$100,001–$200,000	$2000 + 3.5% over $100,001
$200,001–$300,000	$5500 + 4% over $200,001
$300,001–$500,000	$9500 + 5.5% over $300,001
$500,001–$1,000,000	$20,500 + 5.75% over $500,001
$1 million	$49,250 + 6.75% over $1 million

NORTHERN TERRITORY

FOR PROPERTY VALUES up to $500,000 the following formula is used: Amount payable = $(0.065 \times V2) + 21V$ where V = (assessable value) / 1000. For property values over $500,000, the stamp duty is charged at a rate of 5.4% of the amount.

EXAMPLES

IF YOU PURCHASE a property with a stamp duty applicable value of $300,000, the stamp duty for each state would be:

$8975 (Queensland) $8990 (New South Wales)

$9500 (Australia Capital Territory) $9550 (Tasmania)

$12,150 (Northern Territory) $10,700 (Western Australia)

$11,330 (South Australia) $13,660 (Victoria)

Now it's time to start working out a budget for running your actual property. The following are expense categories for you to take into consideration:

RECURRING COSTS

- Property expenses

- Mortgage interest

- Council rates

- Building and landlord insurance

- Repairs and maintenance

- Annual termite inspections and pest sprays

- Letting fees and property management fees

- Body corporation fees (if applicable)

- Cleaning (if applicable)

- Mowing and garden upkeep (if applicable)

- Income

- Rent received

- Tax credits / income tax variation

IT IS IMPORTANT to figure in these fees when calculating your rental yield. I would suggest making a budget for the year for each property. Using a table, such as the following example, is probably the easiest method. Please note that the repairs are only an estimate. You will not know your actual costs until you perform maintenance, but I recommend that you include an estimated amount in your budget.

ITEM						MONTH DUE					
J	F	M	A	M	J	J	A	S	O	N	D

EXPENSES

Loan

J	F	M	A	M	J	J	A	S	O	N	D
1670	1670	1670	1670	1670	1670	1670	1670	1670	1670	1670	1670

Rates

J	F	M	A	M	J	J	A	S	O	N	D
					1600						

Insurance

J	F	M	A	M	J	J	A	S	O	N	D
					570						

Repairs

J	F	M	A	M	J	J	A	S	O	N	D
		250		250		250		250			

Pest

J	F	M	A	M	J	J	A	S	O	N	D
		250									

Letting

J	F	M	A	M	J	J	A	S	O	N	D
		260									

M/Fees

J	F	M	A	M	J	J	A	S	O	N	D
90	90	90	90	90	90	90	90	90	90	90	90

TOTALS

J	F	M	A	M	J	J	A	S	O	N	D
1760	1760	2520	1760	2010	3930	2010	1760	2010	1760	1760	1760

ITEM						MONTH DUE					
J	F	M	A	M	J	J	A	S	O	N	D

INCOME

Rent *

J	F	M	A	M	J	J	A	S	O	N	D
1260	1260	1260	1260	1260	1260	1260	1260	1260	1260	1260	1260

Tax Variat. #

J	F	M	A	M	J	J	A	S	O	N	D
300	300	300	300	300	300	300	300	300	300	300	300

TOTALS

J	F	M	A	M	J	J	A	S	O	N	D
1560	1560	1560	1560	1560	1560	1560	1560	1560	1560	1560	1560

*Rent will increase every six months to two years, depending on market.
#Tax variation will alter each year depending on income and expenses.

NOTE: This table shows a negative geared property. Another consideration for tax benefits is depreciation. This table does not take into account the depreciation that is deductible against the property. Depreciation rates are based on the age of the building, renovations, and inclusion. Some depreciation schedules could allow a deductible rate of around $7000 to $12,000 in the first year.

These tables are a simple formula to keep track of the income and expenses of your investment property. Readily available through property industry specific software are even more detailed forms, which offer even more detail about depreciation, CPI, capital growth, and income growth information. You can use these forms to predict the future growth of your property, and to hold costs to an optimal level.

> *Destiny is not a matter of chance; it is a matter of choice.*
> *– William Jennings Bryan (1860 – 1925),*
> *American Lawyer and Politician*

NEGOTIATING THE PURCHASE

ONCE YOU FIND the right property, it is time to start your negotiations. Buying and selling property is very much a people business. When a casual observer looks at real estate negotiations, it may seem that there is always a winner and a loser – someone gets the property, and someone else gives it up. But that is not necessarily the case. Each party in a real estate deal has a list of wants and a list of needs. As a buyer, the reason for negotiating in real estate is to get all of your needs and most of your wants met. This is also true of the seller.

Unfortunately, there are unknowns when purchasing any home. This means you must do your due diligence or research fully. The home must have various inspections and a valuation done. This can be complicated if the house is still on the market and other buyers are actively looking at it. I always recommend that the buyer make an offer on a property they are interested in, and then include what are known as 'subject to' clauses in that offer, pending the outcome of due diligence. This accomplishes two things. First, it gives the seller an in-hand offer from a serious buyer, so that the seller can confidently take it off the market. Second, it gives the buyer the ability to accomplish due diligence without fear of losing the property, and also gives the buyer a way out if things are not as they appear.

Most contracts in business are simple, upfront transactions. The price is set and agreed upon, and then the paperwork is signed. Both parties are liable to fulfil their portion of the agreed-upon obligations. If either party attempts to renegotiate any point, the other party can negate the original offer and acceptance. However, real estate is different.

Real estate contracts regularly contain specific clauses that allow renegotiation in limited areas. For example, a real estate contract may allow a buyer to get a building and termite inspection report completed on the property. After the buyer receives the report, they will have the option to ask the seller to repair any items that have been found by the inspector that are in need of repair, or even to reduce the agreed-upon sale price. The seller, under the contract, has the right to either repair what the buyer has asked for or deny the buyer's request completely. If the seller denies any requests from the buyer under this clause or condition, the buyer has the right to either take the property as it is or to withdraw from the sale completely prior to the clause date expiring. Property is complex, and it's ill advised to circumvent due diligence or to not include a contingency clause.

Contingencies are a part of property investing, and so are renegotiations, but only in limited areas and according to the contract. It is astounding how many people sign on the dotted line and yet never read their contracts. As an investor, you must read every item, and when you are buying property, you must include any contingency that you think might affect the outcome of the purchase.

You don't want to be struggling with challenges that could have been prevented, or pay more than a home might actually be worth due to your own short-sightedness. While I know that contracts and legalese are sleep-inducing at times, they are very important to your future as a property investor. So don't take short cuts, and make sure you get the best deal possible.

Don't be hesitant to make an offer that is in your best interest. That is what the seller is doing, after all! The whole idea of negotiating is to present your want list to the seller and use that as a starting point. You don't want to give away more than necessary, and oftentimes, the seller will come down in price much further than you anticipated.

LOVER'S LEAP

ONE FINAL WORD of caution: once you make an offer on a house, it is easy to become emotionally attached to the property. In other words, you fall in love. This removes your objectivity as an investor and can get you into trouble. Often people find themselves with properties that have significant structural challenges, or that just don't make sense for their portfolio – but still they want them anyway. This not only creates a situation where they've make a poor investment decision, but it can affect their ability to invest in other properties for months or even years to come. Always look before you leap, and remember – investors never fall in love unless the numbers add up.

QUITTING YOUR DAY JOB

ONE OF THE main wishes or goals on peoples' lists is to make enough money from their property investments to replace their income. While this is entirely possible, I would caution you not to do so prematurely. It is important to remember that cash flow is king, and your regular job provides a good deal of that in a steady fashion. You must be able to weather the inevitable ups and downs in the rental market with significant savings in place. It is also important to be aware that your lender might become nervous if your steady cash flow from regular employment ceases. This could mean they no longer will loan you the amounts necessary to keep investing in more properties – or worse, they may call some of your loans due. Hang on to your day job until you are experienced and have substantial cash on hand.

The properties you have purchased will determine how long you should keep your day job. If all the properties you purchase in your portfolio are positive geared, and the income is enough for you to enjoy your lifestyle, then great. However, I would always allow in your budget for times when any of the properties may be vacant.

Another strategy of investors is to keep purchasing properties and hold them for around ten years, or until they at least double in value. After such a period, they sell half of them, pay out the mortgages on the other half, pay their capital gains taxes, and then live on the full rental income from the half they still own. If you do this, always take into account any down time of vacancies and any maintenance that the properties may need.

CHAPTER 8
MY PROPERTY

1.   Work from a checklist when evaluating properties.

2.   Be sure to check what fixtures and fittings are included in the sale.

3.   Know the fees involved in purchasing property.

4.   Don't hesitate to make an offer in your best interest.

5.   Resist the urge to fall in love with a property.

6.   Think ahead and include any 'subject to' clauses you might deem necessary.

7.   Hang on to your day job until you gain plenty of experience and have substantial cash on hand.

MY ACTION PLAN AND NOTES

_____

_____

_____

_____

_____

_____

_____

_____

_____

_____

CHAPTER
9

MY RENTAL:

HOW TO RENT MY PROPERTY

TO TENANTS

MY RENTAL:
HOW TO RENT MY PROPERTY TO
TENANTS

Learn how to separate the majors and the minors. A lot of people don't
do well simply because they major in minor things.
— Jim Rohn, Business Philosopher

Managing your own rental property can become overwhelming if you have more than a few properties. Some first-time investors choose to go it alone on the first one or two to save money. However, it will quickly become apparent to most that it makes good sense to employ the services of a professional property manager. While some may balk at paying the fees, it is usually only around 7 to 9 per cent of the rent. This amount can be insignificant in comparison to issues that may arise in rental legalities, and is well worth it not to receive phone calls in the middle of night from a tenant.

If you decide you want to manage your own rental property, it requires you to have intense organizational and management skills, as well as knowledge of state tenancy legislation. You will also need a big dose of communication skills, as rentals are all about dealing with various types of people. There is a misconception that if you manage your own investment properties you do not have to follow Residential Tenancies legislation. This is completely untrue. You are still required to complete all legislation documentation and hold all money according to regulations. Most states have websites that enable private landlords to print tenancies forms at no charge.

Once you decide to become a landlord, you have some responsibilities to provide a liveable and clean property for the tenants to occupy. It is good to have a checklist of items that you clean or replace after each tenant vacates the property. This ensures a measurable level of cleanliness and order for the next tenant. Following is a sample that either you or your property manager can use to ensure that all areas are addressed:

ENTIRE HOUSE

- Dust

- Vacuum

- Shampoo carpet

- Mop all floors, and treat or wax if needed

- Wipe down all walls

- Patch all holes

- Paint when and where necessary

- Clean light fixtures – wash fixtures

- Clean windows

- Replace torn screens

- Check all windows for ease of opening

- Check all smoke detectors

- Oil door hinges as needed

KITCHEN

- Thoroughly clean all appliances

- Check garbage disposal seals

- Vacuum bottom of refrigerator and around compressor (if applicable)

- Replace exhaust fan filters

- Clean all cabinets and replace contact paper if needed

- Clean ovens and drip pans on stove

- Replace any broken appliance bulbs

BATHROOMS

- Clean and disinfect

- Remove soap scum

- Replace shower curtain

- Remove all mildew

- Vacuum exhaust fan – replace if broken

- Clean out medicine cabinet

- Check under vanity for leakage

- Check toilet for proper flushing

- Tighten towel racks

THIS IS BY no means an exhaustive list, but I'm sure you get the idea. This allows someone to investigate every part of the rental and fix what is broken, or report what they can't fix for repairs. This not only provides the next tenant a nice place, but it also ensures a good amount of continued upkeep and maintenance. Your rental does not have to be grandiose, but it does need to justify the rental price. So, if you have broken appliances, fix them. If your property needs an air conditioner, buy it. Don't expect your tenant to be happy in a home you wouldn't live in. Present the property in pristine condition, and you will be more likely to achieve top dollar in rent.

When you are ready, you need to advertise the property for rent. You can do this by placing signs in the yard or running ads in the newspaper. You can also use the Internet. Once the ads are out, be prepared to answer phone calls, and block out the time necessary to show the property. This can be a pain, especially if you are renting several properties, but it cannot be skipped or handled by someone else at this point, especially if this is your only property. You are the best judge of the right person for your house. You can talk to them, ask questions about their lives, and get a sense of the kind of people they are. Look at their vehicle. Is it clean and tidy? If so, they will probably treat your property the same. Above all, trust your intuition. If something doesn't seem right, don't be afraid to say no.

It is also important to be ready for any repairs or maintenance from the first day a tenant enters your property. You don't want to have to scramble to find someone at a moment's notice. If you are managing the properties yourself and are very handy, you can certainly do repairs yourself. However, few people are truly proficient unless they do it full time. Some landlords allow tenants to make needed repairs and deduct the expenses from their rent.

Insist that all tenants comply with your rental policies. This can be difficult to monitor, depending on your policies. It is good to drive by the property regularly to see if there are any obvious violations. However, there is a fine line between watching over your property and annoying your tenants. They have a right to live in peace, even though it is your investment. One way to sidestep this challenge is to hire someone to conduct six-month 'maintenance checks' of the property. These are scheduled inspections of the home. This person can be your eyes and ears, and can let you know whether the tenants are taking care of your property. They can also tell how many people are living in the home, and spot any potential violations of your rental agreement.

Always supervise repair and maintenance work! By allowing someone else to do repairs and sending an invoice, you have no idea how well they are doing the job. If the person you hired is doing a poor job on repairs, it can eventually cost you more money, not to mention the possibility of severe detrimental effects to the property.

Collect your rents in an organised and established fashion. Many private landlords use a post office box. This prevents tenants from coming to your house. It also allows the investor privacy and the assurance that there won't be a tenant at your door at four in the morning wanting you to do some repairs. The payment policies and procedures should be clearly stated in your rental agreement, as well as any penalties for rent arrears. One mistake investors often make when they start out is to be too lenient and allow tenants to skip a payment or to pay late. This does not help the tenant or investor, and causes major stress to both parties. Stick to your agreement and insist that the tenant uphold their part of the legal agreement. It is also smart to write into the lease that late payments and returned cheques will be considered rent arrears.

WHY EMPLOY A PROFESSIONAL PROPERTY MANAGER?

FROM MY YEARS in real estate, I can tell you that when landlords manage their properties themselves, they can get themselves into a fair bit of trouble. Here are some points that present challenges to a landlord when managing their own investment property:

- Legislation

- Tenants who know their rights

- Renting to family and friends

LEGISLATION

TENANCY LEGISLATION VARIES from state to state in Australia. Although the overall principle is similar, the laws are still very different. When I moved from Victoria to Queensland and started investing in real estate in the new area, I started learning the legislation all over again. It did not really help that I had worked for ten years under Victoria's rental legislation. While the overall concepts were similar, the specific forms, lengths of notices, and types of procedures needed for each situation were all new. For example, one state may allow you to give a tenant notice to vacate the premises if their rent is seven days in arrears. In contrast, another state may require you to issue two breach notices when a tenant is seven days in arrears, and then if they fail to pay their rent, you can issue a notice to leave. There also are different laws that dictate increases in rent. Tenancy legislation in Queensland allows you increase rent after thirty days' notice, provided that the rent increase is issued prior to the tenant's lease expiring, but the increase is not to occur until the lease does expire. It may require as much as sixty days' notice if the tenant is on a periodic lease. But another state may require you to give a tenant sixty days' notice to increase the rent regardless of when the notice is issued to the tenant.

I have actually witnessed landlords attending tribunal hearings after they issued tenants a notice to leave based on rent arrears. When I viewed a particular landlord present their case to the judge (or referee) they were required to submit all their evidence to support their case along with evidence to show that they have followed the legislation in managing the property and serving the notice to lease to the tenant. When the referee asked the landlord how many days extra in the notice were allowed for postage days (most legislations in Australia requires the landlord to add postage days to notice periods, for example, adding three days extra to the notice), the landlord was required to supply a copy of his registered post receipt to prove the day of service or the day he sent the notice. The landlord sent the notice to leave registered post on a Friday, and allowed two postage days. As per requirements, if a notice to leave is posted on Friday, the referee expects you to add an extra three days for delivery of the mail. Because this landlord only allowed two days, the case was thrown out, and the referee refused to go any further with the landlord's application for possession. Because of the complexities of legislation, private landlords can easily fail to meet all the requirements.

TENANTS WHO KNOW THEIR RIGHTS

RENTING IS SUCH a common living arrangement today that most people rent a property at some stage of their lives. This being the case, many tenants know their rights, and they are also supplied with full rights and duties booklets when they first move into a property. There are also free advisory boards available to tenants if a tenant receives a notice for vacating, rent increases, entry notices, or for any other reason. They are able to seek full advice from these boards, and can sometimes receive legal assistance if they choose to dispute a notice.

Agents can communicate with the tenancy advisory boards weekly and monthly to negotiate notices issued. The advisory board may ring the agent and ask that the tenant's rent not be increased by twenty dollars, but instead by five. Most of the time, if the legislation is followed perfectly, agents are able to enforce the notice. The purpose of these boards is to help tenants understand their rights and to assist them in understanding the legislation, and also to negotiate with the landlords/agents on behalf of the tenants to prevent tribunal attendances. These boards are quite helpful, and do prevent situations from expanding into tribunal hearings, which obviously is a better option for all involved.

LANDLORDS RENTING TO FRIENDS AND FAMILY

THIS IS A common situation that results in many families falling out and friendships ending. I have picked the pieces up many times from landlords who decided to mix their business with helping their family and friends. I strongly urge any landlord who is considering renting a property to a family member or a friend to have the agreement fully documented and decided upon prior to the lease commencing, including rent increases and rent arrears procedure.

I have watched a landlord rent a property to his struggling brother and his family at $200 per week, which was probably $20 per week under market. Then, three years later, when comparative properties were renting for $300 per week, the brother was still only paying $200. The brother was behind because his car had blown up, and he had to pay $2000 to repair it. The poor brother renting the property knew his landlord brother would understand if he fell behind in his rent. Besides, he figured, if his brother had enough money to own a rental property, he certainly had enough money carry him through difficult financial times.

How many people can relate to this story, or to similar situations? Think about it: for a full year, this owner received $100 less per week than the market rent, which meant that the landlord missed out on at least $5000 per year. This could have helped him purchase another investment property, or allowed him to take his family on a great holiday each year.

Some renters have the mentality that if people own a rental property, they must be wealthy and can afford to weather shortfalls in rent, or that they can renovate or add additional features to their rental property at any time. This is a common misconception, as many people who take the initiative to buy investment properties generally forgo a luxury in their life to do so. It may be that they only go out to dinner once a month rather than twice a week. Whatever an investor has altered in his or her life to purchase a property, I can guarantee that initially, they do change something in order to get ahead later in their life. As I mentioned in an earlier chapter, I lived in a unit that was the size of a hotel room when I first started buying investment properties. This was no sacrifice for me, as I had a plan and a goal, and for me the tiny apartment was a choice I made to achieve my goal.

THE TENANT AND LANDLORD RELATIONSHIP

Get around the right people. Associate with positive,
goal-oriented people who encourage and inspire you
– Brian Tracy, Business Philosopher

I DO NOT mean to imply that the tenant and the landlord are enemies. As with buyers and sellers, they need each other in order to achieve their goals. Without tenants renting an investor's property, the investor will fail in his or her financial freedom plan.

People want to live in as nice a home as possible, no matter what their income level. They also want to be treated kindly, and want their concerns answered in a timely fashion. All of these points are important to understand and to be aware of constantly. Landlords who treat tenants with disdain or disrespect are only hurting themselves. The people living in your rental property are taking care of one of your quickly appreciating assets, and they can help you if you let them.

I have had clients over the years who rented a very plain property out to tenants. During the tenancy, the tenants invested huge amounts of time into the garden, and basically fully landscaped the front and rear yards. They also paved an outdoor entertaining area and made new curtains for the windows. I watched one particular property increase by $30,000 simply by the tenants caring about what their home looked like.

Tenants like these are invaluable, and any landlord who does not appreciate these types of tenants should not be a landlord. I have known of 'perfect' tenants asking their landlord to spend a few hundred dollars on plants and material for them. The landlord flatly refused. Needless to say, the tenants felt very despondent, and frankly, these types of landlords do not deserve tenants like this.

Agents can experience difficult landlords, too – it is not always the tenant that proves difficult. Often I have had landlords who are unrealistic and unreasonable in their approach to their tenants. I urge all landlords who have exceptional tenants to treat them well, as tenants can make or break your investment property.

LANDLORD'S INSURANCE

ANOTHER IMPORTANT AREA to think about before renting is landlord's insurance. I mentioned the importance of insurance previously, and I'll expand on the idea here. Even though this type of insurance is very expensive, I'm amazed that less than 60 per cent of investors carry it. A good policy will cover a multitude of possibilities, and can be a lifesaver when bad things happen. Some of the items that can be covered include the following:

- Accidental or intentional damage by tenants, as well as lost rental income during repairs

- Legal liability

- Theft by tenants

- Loss of rent

- Rent default if a tenant leaves without paying rent

- Rent default during an eviction

- Rent default if a tenant stays and does not pay

- Full building and compulsory third-party liability

- Legal and court costs

SHOULD THINGS GO badly, or should a tenant skip town, this policy can guard your wallet from a substantial hit. Your policy should include building insurance, contents insurance, and landlord's insurance. Many companies combine these three types into one umbrella policy, which is known as a landlord's policy. Some have separate policies for each, but it is usually more cost effective to have the combined policy. Most insurance companies will ask for copies of the original lease agreement, condition report, and tenant credit checks. If you are unable to provide these to the insurance company, they may refuse to pay out on any tenant breach claims, as some policies have in small print that the landlord must comply with all legislation to validate their insurance policy.

> *The secret of business is to know something*
> *that nobody else knows.*
> *– Aristotle Socrates Onassis (1906 – 75),*
> *Greek Shipping Magnate*

PROPERTY MANAGERS

IF YOU FIND that rental management is not for you, consider hiring the services of a professional property manager. Ideally, you should look for someone who is experienced and knowledgeable about the rental market in the area. If you feel like the hassle from managing your own investments isn't worth it, try outsourcing the duties to a professional management company.

Property management is a specialised industry, and a good property manager can benefit your wealth creation. Over the years, I have told property managers that looking after a client's property is the same as them handing you $300,000 cash and asking you to increase the amount over the years you look after it. Looking after a $300,000 property is no different from looking after $300,000 cash. I think that when property managers realise that the house their client has entrusted to them is the same as giving them cash to increase in value, it gives them a more realistic idea of how important their role is with their clients.

Selecting a property manager is just like conducting a job interview. You need to get on well with your property manager, and you need to be able to trust him or her to act in your best interest. The relationship you have with your property manager is so important because he or she is your eyes and ears. This is especially true if you are located in another town or city, as long-distance management of rental property can be difficult and time consuming. In this case, it is simply not practical for you to manage the property.

Some questions you might ask a potential property manager are the following:

HOW LONG HAVE YOU BEEN IN THE INDUSTRY?

JUST BECAUSE PROPERTY managers hold the legal licenses to manage property does not mean that they necessarily know what they are doing. It can take years to understand and experience the complexities of the industry, and experience is the key. When I first started, I did my schooling and applied for my license, and I thought, 'Now I know what I am doing'. But looking back, there was no way I fully understood everything that can go wrong with rental properties and how to overcome particular situations. Time was my mentor and enthusiasm was my key to success. I had a burning desire to be the best property manager in the area where I worked, and this did pay off. I eventually was very well known, and received weekly referrals from existing clients.

Lord, grant that I may desire more than I can accomplish
– Michelangelo (1474 – 1564),
Italian Sculptor, Painter, and Writer

ONE OTHER POINT: speak to your property manager and evaluate his or her attitude. The property manager may have been working for five plus years, but is he or she still enthusiastic about the business? Sometimes experience can work as a disadvantage: an experienced person may no longer have the passion for the job.

HOW LONG HAVE YOU WORKED WITH YOUR AGENCY?

IT IS GOOD to know that your property manager is settled in the company he or she works for, as you don't want to build a relationship with a property manager who moves to another agency six months down the track. A consistent employee provides consistent service to you.

WHAT DO YOU THINK OF TENANTS?

THIS MAY SOUND strange, but if your property manager talks about tenants with contempt, chances are he or she will treat them poorly. This will result in your property being vacant regularly, which, of course, mean loss of rent. A good property manager understands that tenants are his or her clients too, and although it is the landlord that pays the wages, without tenants there will be no commission with which to pay wages. I have also heard of property managers who favour the tenants too much. There is a fine line between having good relationships with tenants and being too friendly with them. I work on the theory that property managers must act in a professional manner toward tenants and respect them, but not become too friendly, as they may have to give them notice to leave one day if they fall behind in their rent.

CAN YOU SUPPLY ME WITH THE WRITTEN PROPOSAL?

A WRITTEN PROPOSAL of what the agency services are will quickly show you how professional the agency is. If a property manager meets you and says, 'Yes, I can rent out your property', and yet is unable to provide you any written information regarding the services and benefits to using their agency, this could mean that he or she will take a blasé approach and manage your property. You want a property manager who can show you that they will manage your property in a professional and systematic way.

ARE YOU PROACTIVE?
IF SO, IN WHAT WAY?

IT IS GOOD to know that even if legislation only requires a few routine internal inspections per year, the property manager nonetheless drives past the properties every so often to check how they look. So much can happen in a matter of months with a property, and you need your property manager to be on the ball.

You also want to know that your property manager acts promptly to take care of any issues concerning your property. You would hate to hear that your tenants have gone without power for two days because the property manager has been 'too busy' to call an electrician.

HOW MANY PROPERTIES DO YOU
MANAGE, AND WHAT SUPPORT
DO YOU HAVE?

IT IS DIFFICULT to receive good service from a property manager who is managing too many properties. They only have one set of hands, and an overworked property manager is usually stressed and not performing at his or her best. I would suggest that the maximum number of properties that a property manager could look after is 180 to 200 – provided they have a support staff. Many property management businesses have an accounts department and a maintenance department, and also assistance with paperwork or arrears in their business.

DO YOU HAND OUT KEYS TO
POTENTIAL TENANTS?

THIS IS ONE of my pet peeves, as I think it is risky, unprofessional, and wasted time in getting to know your potential tenant. I would like to know who has insurance coverage for handing out keys to a potential tenant who cuts a set of keys and later uses them to rob the property when it is occupied. Property managers only hand out keys if they are too lazy or lack time to conduct property inspections themselves, in which case they give out the keys to future renters to inspect the property on their own. This act only puts future tenants at risk of being robbed, or, worse, allows a possible litigation suit against the owner for not ensuring a safe environment to the renters.

It is also unprofessional. A real estate sales person never hands out keys to a potential buyer, so why is it any different with a potential tenant? At the end of the day, a property manager's job is to sell the rental property to the tenant, not to just hand out keys.

It is also a missed opportunity for the property manager to get to know the tenant. I have picked many a tenant during the time that I showed them through the property, as long as my decision could be confirmed through rental checks. I have also met tenants on the property who I knew would not be suitable at all, even though their applications read extremely well. A property manager needs to spend time with the tenants at the inspection, and then process their applications with care.

DO YOU HAVE YOUR OWN INVESTMENT PROPERTY?

I LIKE TO know if my property manager has investment property. I find that when this is the case, the property manager is more aware and understanding of my needs as a landlord, and will do more work for me. To me, a property manager who is an investor is the ideal manager. If a property manager understands that the rent must be paid on time for me to meet all of my financial responsibilities, I am 90 per cent of the way there with a successful investment property.

WHAT TYPES OF CHECKS DO YOU DO ON APPLICANTS?

THERE ARE MANY tenant check databases available for property managers today to use to check out a tenant's past performance. Just as a bank checks us for our credit rating, there are companies that property managers can subscribe to so they can check to see if a person has left money owing at a previous rental property. This is not foolproof, as many bad tenants will rent from landlords who manage their own properties. This is because private landlords do not access these types of databases, and are generally left with huge amounts of money still owed and little recourse to obtain the debt from the tenant.

You can screen the best candidates for your rental by requiring written applications with credit and employment references. It is important that all applications be written, and that you retain records of the applications of all of the people who rent your property. And don't forget to check references! If applicants give you disconnected phone numbers and addresses that don't exist, then they obviously should not be trusted. One word of advice on this subject: full credit checks can be expensive, and they don't always reveal a poor tenant. Even if someone has a great credit background, they can vandalise your house. Take some time to talk to the people you are considering.

WHAT ARE YOUR FEES?

AGENTS CHARGE A management fee and usually a letting fee for initially starting a tenant in your property. Check to see if there are any other fees, as some agents charge for taking photographs, conducting inspections, attending a tribunal hearing, and renewing tenant leases. When you first give your property to an agent to manage, all of the agent's fees should be listed on the initial agreement. Remember, the cheapest agent may not be the best.

WHAT DO YOUR OTHER CLIENTS SAY ABOUT YOU AS A PROPERTY MANAGER?

ASK IF THE property manager has any testimonials from existing clients. These testimonials may be in the form of cards, emails, and letters. If a client is happy enough with their property manager to provide them with a testimonial or reference, then chances are you will be happy with their service.

PROPERTY MANAGERS: OVERVIEW OF THEIR SERVICES

Manage by objectives. Tell people exactly what you want them to do and then get out of their way.
– Brian Tracy, Business Philosopher

PROPERTY MANAGEMENT SPECIALISTS look after all areas of the rental of your investment property, and can make one of the more involved areas of property investment a lot smoother for you. Their roles are comprehensive and include:

MARKET RENT VALUE

PROPERTY MANAGERS HAVE many resources available to them to help them determine the market value of your rental property. One of the main ways market rent is assessed is by looking at other rental properties in the area and the facilities that these properties have to offer. Marketable rent is determined by features such as number of bedrooms, number of living areas, air conditioners, dishwashers, vehicle accommodations, shedding, age of home, décor, and storage. Many property managers also have access to databases that help them assess the market.

ADVERTISING

ONE OF THE major forms of advertising for rentals properties today is the Internet; it is the quickest and most efficient way to get your property out in the market. Most agents subscribe to real-estate-based websites that are common in the industry. Any prospective tenants looking for properties to rent will view these websites to source a suitable property to rent. If an agent lists your property on the Internet, this may cost them between $30 and $60. However, if you listed the property as a private landlord, it could cost you $250 plus. Because agents pay monthly fees for these services, they receive each property listing at a cheaper rate than someone who would only list once.

SOURCING TENANTS

MOST PROPERTY MANAGERS keep a list of potential tenants who are looking for properties. Therefore, when your property is vacant, they may be able to source a new tenant in a matter of days. Also, existing tenants refer other tenants to good property managers, and this is an excellent method of sourcing good tenants.

PREPARING DOCUMENTATION

THE DOCUMENTATION INVOLVED in leasing a property is extensive, and can consist of twenty to thirty pages of tenant agreements, condition reports, bond lodgements, agency policies, and procedures on matters such as rent arrears and routine inspections. Also, by law, property managers are required to provide rights and duties information to tenants relating to the state legislation.

In most states, tenants are asked to pay a bond, which is usually four weeks rent or the calendar monthly rent amount. Landlords are required by law to provide the tenant a condition report of the property. Obviously, all landlords want a bond paid, and they definitely want a full and comprehensive condition report completed on their property. A condition report is prepared to ensure that the condition of the property remains the same during the renter's tenancy, excluding what is called 'fair wear and tear'. Fair wear and tear is usually wear that a property will have regardless of who lives there. For example, carpets can wear thin in the high-traffic areas of rooms and become worn looking, or the paintwork can look patchy due to the walls being washed in the usual course of living in a home. A landlord cannot claim compensation for wearing carpet or other areas that the tribunal or court deems to be classed as fair wear and tear. This is a landlord's responsibility, and is part of the natural course of owning an investment property that the property is bound to experience wear and from time to time, requiring the landlord to replace floor coverings or repaint.

The condition report will document the fixtures, fittings, and any imperfections with the property from room to room. For example, a lounge room section of the condition report would read

- Walls – Two hooks on north wall, small plaster patch size, 10 cm circle, Panasonic split system air condition mounted on south wall.

- Floor coverings – Professional steam-cleaned carpet, small brown mark size of 5 cm circle in middle of room.

- Kitchen – Westinghouse dishwasher, hardwired timber clock on south wall, two hooks south wall, four hooks east wall, Westinghouse hot plates and wall oven cleaned.

GENERALLY, A CONDITION report will list everything in the property room by room, and in each room it will cover all of the features of that room, including

- Floor coverings

- Walls

- Ceilings

- Windows

- Window coverings

- Light fittings

- Power points / TV points

  Bathrooms, kitchens, and laundries have additional spaces for

- Baths

- Showers

- Vanities

- Cooking facilities

- Electrical appliances

- Cupboards

- Bench tops

- Refrigerators

- Microwaves

- Sinks

- Clothes dryers

- Washing machine taps

BOND LODGEMENT

IN MOST STATES, tenants' bonds are required to be lodged within a short period with the relevant state bond authority. A misconception that many landlords have is that the bond belongs to them as the landlord, but this is not correct. The purpose of a bond is to ensure that when a tenant vacates a property, the tenant pays all the rent outstanding, and presents the property back in the same condition, excluding 'fair wear and tear'. If the tenant fails to do so, then a landlord can make a claim against the tenant's bond. The bond is lodged with the relevant authority in trust for the tenant and belongs to the tenant at all times, unless a claim is made at the end of the lease.

ACCOUNTING AND RECORD KEEPING

THE ACCOUNTS DEPARTMENT in a property management business can save you a lot of money in the reporting they provide – versus what you would pay your accountant to spend endless hours checking your income and expenses. Most agencies provide monthly statements to landlords that detail how much rent was received and when, as well as maintenance and management fees. At the end of the financial year, most real estate programs are able to provide landlords with a summary of their yearly income and expenses.

The accounts department can pay the council rates on your behalf out of the rent, along with any maintenance invoices. This can make life easy for you in that you don't have to remember to pay council rates on the property – the agency takes care of this for you.

MAINTENANCE

PROPERTY MANAGERS HAVE a list of tradespeople who are available to complete all areas of maintenance on a client's property. These tradespeople are fully insured, which protects you as the landlord if anything goes wrong. They will usually be competitive with price, as tradespeople receive the majority of their work from agents – and this kind of work is consistent for them. If the agencies look after tradespeople with regular payment of invoices, they will be available very quickly to complete repairs, therefore ensuring happy tenants.

RENOVATIONS/ALTERATIONS

PROPERTY MANAGERS ARE very much in touch with what their tenants want, and with what will achieve a higher rental income for a landlord. Landlords often need to freshen up their properties with paint and floor coverings, and they may still have a few extra dollars to spend in another area. Talk to your property manager, as the new garden you were thinking about may not increase the rental return of your property. You may be better off spending this on air conditioning, as this could increase you're the amount of rent by twenty dollars per week. Your property manager will know where best to spend a few dollars, and will also be able to help you in getting quotes. They have the contacts for all areas of property improvement, and sometimes will be able to achieve a better price for you.

RENTAL ARREARS

AS I PREVIOUSLY mentioned, there are many requirements in each state to follow with rent arrear procedures, and property managers are up to date with all the relevant documentation and legalities required when this occurs. Chasing a tenant for rent is one of the worst jobs, and can be uncomfortable for all concerned. This is one area where a property manager is worth his or her weight in gold. Most agencies have a procedure they follow when the tenant falls one or two days in arrears, and they monitor this daily.

ROUTINE INSPECTIONS

EACH STATE HAS different laws regarding the number of times a property can be inspected each year during a tenancy, and it can vary from biyearly to quarterly. I would recommend these inspections be conducted as regularly as allowed, as you will quickly know of any potential challenges. This also gives the owner an idea of how the property is wearing and what may need attention in the coming months or year.

RENT REVIEWS

RENT REVIEWS ARE important to enable you to achieve the maximum return from your investment. If you are able to increase the rent every six or twelve months, it will tremendously benefit your cash flow. Keep in mind that the property can only be increased to its market value. Just because we experience two interest rate hikes in a six-month period does not necessarily mean that the rent can be increased each time. Interest rate increases and a rise in council rates are some of the areas that investors need to take into consideration as some of the possible expenses that will occur during the life of your investment property.

LEASE RENEWALS

IT IS ALWAYS a good idea to keep your property manager informed of any changes you are considering with your property. For instance, you may decide to sell a property for whatever reason. However, if you have a tenant on a fixed leased for another ten months, the chances of selling your property to an owner-occupier is limited, as they will not want to purchase a property they cannot live in for another ten months. This therefore limits your buyer's pool and can hinder a sale for you.

Having tenants on the lease is like fixing your bank interest rate. You know that a tenant will be in the property for the term of their lease, and that you have a consistent monthly rent coming in to pay for the property. Fixed leases are a great source of peace of mind, but always consider the length of the lease. I think six-month only renewal periods are long enough in a market that is hot and increasing in rental value every few months. If you have a tenant fixed for a long lease of two years, and over that two-year period the market significantly increases by 10 to 20 per cent each year, your property may be $50 to $100 under market rent at the expiration of the lease.

TRIBUNAL/COURT APPEARANCES

Difficulties come not to obstruct, but to instruct.
– Brian Tracy, Business Philosopher

IF YOU HAVE ever experienced any court attendance, you know that this is a daunting experience. But in the world of property management, it is a given that at some stage you will attend one for some reason. I don't think I need to explain further the benefit of having a professional property manager acting on your behalf in a court or tribunal hearing.

VACATING TENANTS

WHEN A TENANT gives notice to vacate a premise, the property manager will check whether they are on a periodic lease. If they are on a fixed lease, then this is classed as a lease break, and the tenants can be liable for the rent until a new tenant is sourced. They will also be responsible for the re-letting costs of the property, including advertising and the letting fee.

If the tenant who has given notice is on a periodic lease, then the property manager will check to see if they have given the legislative period required to vacate. Depending on the area where your property is located, your property manager may be able to source a new tenant to commence within twenty-four to forty-eight hours of your current tenant vacating.

When tenants give notice, this is also an important time to review the rent. This is usually when landlords experience a large difference in rent increases, as it is easier to raise the rent between tenants.

The property manager will conduct a full inspection of the property after the tenant has vacated the property. The manager ensures all the keys that were issued to the tenant originally are returned, that the property has been left in a clean and tidy manner, and that the condition is the same as the entry condition report.

Earlier, we discussed the importance of talking to a solicitor to be sure that your rental agreements and knowledge of the laws governing rental property are up to date. While the idea of being a landlord can seem a little intimidating, there is nothing about it that is hard. However, it is time consuming. But for the beginning investor who likes to be involved, that is part of the fun of real estate.

LEGISLATION CHANGES

AS WITH ANY governed industry, rental legislation is amended from time to time, and the relevant authorities change the legal forms and documentation. It is a property manager's job to keep informed of all these changes, and he or she does this with industry-related memberships and subscriptions to real estate organizations. If a landlord fails to adhere to changes, the tenants can seek compensation if the law is not followed correctly.

A recent change we experienced in Queensland involved smoke alarms. All properties, regardless of age, must have compliant smoke alarms installed in them, and they must be cleaned and serviced throughout the year. Failure to do so can result in the landlord being fined. We had to implement a new procedure to include smoke alarm checks in every rental property. The legislation states that not only do the smoke alarms have to be checked throughout the year, but they must also be checked prior to a new tenant moving into the property, regardless of whether the alarm was only checked four months earlier.

OTHER BENEFITS

ONE OF THE biggest challenges private landlords face is the emotional aspect of property management. Having a property manager to buffer you from the tenant creates a better business relationship, and also enables you to make decisions based on business rather than emotion. All property investment is emotional, and even the most seasoned landlord can get emotionally involved with their properties and tenants. It will serve you well to step away from the direct management for business reasons.

I would certainly class myself as an experienced real estate professional and property investor, but even I know the emotions that can jump up if you become too involved with the management. Regardless of my experience in real estate and property management, I hand all my properties over to property managers. It is less stressful, and I am able to make all decisions based on business rather than emotion.

A FINAL WORD

PROPERTY MANAGEMENT CAN be very rewarding as you watch your property grow in value, and if you have tenants who help you pay for your investment. Each landlord is different, and depending on your personal preference as to whether you wish to be involved on a limited basis or extensively, I suggest that you find the property manager who best fits your needs. After all, it will be a relationship that is required to withstand the test of time, and you need to have complete faith in your property manager.

Personally, I do not spend my time managing any of my investment properties; I would much rather use my time looking for the next property to buy.

Happy property renting to you, my fellow investor!

CHAPTER 9
MY RENTAL

1. If you have good tenants, treat them like gold.

2. Landlord insurance can save your wallet from a multitude of disasters.

3. Once you own more than a few properties, it makes sense to locate a good property manager.

4. Experience is key when looking for a property manager, and you must find someone you get on with exceptionally well.

5. It is important to understand the laws concerning tenants.

6. A good property manager will evaluate tenants and their applications thoroughly, and check all references.

7. The service of a property manager can relieve you of daily stress in dealing with tenants, and allow you to continue to look for more properties.

8. Beware of the property manager who does not own investment property, as this individual may not have your best interests at heart.

MY ACTION PLAN AND NOTES

_____

_____

_____

_____

_____

_____

_____

_____

_____

_____

_____

CHAPTER
10

MY AUSTRALIAN INVESTMENT:

HOW TO BUY AUSTRALIAN

PROPERTY IF I AM A FOREIGNER

CHAPTER | 10

MY AUSTRALIAN INVESTMENT: HOW TO BUY AUSTRALIAN PROPERTY IF I AM A FOREIGNER

Success is 20% skills and 80% strategy.
– Jim Rohn, Business Philosopher

P roperty is booming in Australia. While other real estate markets around the world have experienced declines, in Australia the outlook remains strong. If you are not an Australian resident and are looking to buy property in Australia, either for investment or to live in, there are several aspects of the real estate buying process that you should understand.

Owner-occupied properties in Australia comprise about 70 per cent of the total housing market, which is on par with the United Kingdom. Because Australia operates under a similar common law structure as the United Kingdom, United States, Canada, Ireland, and New Zealand, the purchasing of property is considered rather straightforward and familiar to individuals from those countries. It is very important to note that any foreigner wishing to buy property in Australia must first have the approval of the Foreign Investment Review Board (FIRB).

THE FOREIGN INVESTMENT REVIEW BOARD (FIRB)

THE FOREIGN INVESTMENT Review Board is the advisory board that reviews all necessary applications for foreign property investment against the requirements of government policy. Policies limit certain types of investments by foreigners, while trying to encourage foreign investment in order to help the Australian economy. To this end, there are certain types of properties that are easier for foreigners to buy, such as new construction, as it encourages growth for local areas.

Prior to seeking out properties, it is important to understand the requirements and forms necessary for FIRB approval in order to be sure the property you choose conforms to the requirements. You can gain a quick overview of these requirements on the FIRB website at www.firb.gov.au. Prospective buyers from certain countries, such as New Zealand and the United States, have been given less strict requirements through legislation. Seeking out a sales agent with experience in dealing with the FIRB can be quite helpful to the foreign investor.

Once you find a property, it is important to insert a clause within the contract that is contingent on gaining FIRB approval. This protects you on the chance that you don't receive approval for some reason. Should you buy a property without approval, you have broken the law, and may be forced to sell it by the FIRB. They may also pass along the information to other governmental entities, which could cause tremendous challenges if you are lodging an application for a visa.

You can buy property in Australia through conventional means – which is to exchange contracts – or you can buy at auction. Both of these avenues have different requirements for foreigners. As I already stated, the conventional route must include a clause that the purchase is contingent upon FIRB approval. Usually this approval can be obtained within thirty days, though it is sometimes longer.

Auctions, however, present a different challenge. The basic premise of the auction is unconditional purchase of the property in question. This, by its very nature, does not allow for a contingency clause concerning FIRB approval. You can advise the board of your intention to purchase a particular property at auction, and they can frequently pre-approve the purchase in about five days. This means you can arrive with FIRB approval in hand should you be the winning bid on that particular property, provided, of course, that this property has been approved by the FIRB. Not all properties are FIRB approved, and it is recommended that you obtain approval prior to committing to any property.

Obviously, there are many types of properties that foreigners may be interested in so purchasing, so I've listed some options to consider.

BUYING A PROPERTY FROM A DEVELOPER

APARTMENTS OR TOWNHOUSES in a proposed development, or in a development that has recently been completed but has not yet been occupied or sold, can be sold to foreign investors as long as the developer applies in advance to allow foreign purchasers. If a foreign citizen buys a property in this way, (often called 'buying off the plan'), the property, once completed, can be leased or rented, sold, or used by the purchaser. However, foreign interests cannot hold more than half the apartments or townhouses in any one development. Before you consider purchasing such an 'off the plan' property, you should ask to see the developer's approval letter to ensure that FIRB approval exists for sales to foreigners, just to ensure that there are not any challenges later.

PURCHASING WITHIN A RESORT

IF THE AUSTRALIAN Treasurer nominates that a particular resort is an Integrated Tourism Resort, then both residences and vacant land can be purchased within that resort by anybody without any FIRB assessment taking place. The seller of any such property would make this status known to all prospective purchasers. To be considered an Integrated Tourism Resort, the development must fulfil certain conditions, such as covering at least fifty hectares of land within defined boundaries, have extensive recreational facilities, and so forth. This offers numerous advantages for foreign purchasers, including the fact that resorts offer some of the most popular properties and have tremendous potential for capital appreciation in a short time. These properties are also quite easy to rent, as they have so many desirable amenities within the resort complex.

COMMERCIAL REAL ESTATE

YOU MUST OBTAIN FIRB approval to purchase existing commercial and non-residential real estate valued at $5 million or more. These purchases are normally approved unless they are considered 'contrary to the national interest'. There may also be different limits if the purchaser is from New Zealand or the United States.

If the commercial property is in the development or redevelopment stage, permission to purchase is usually given, unless the purchase is considered 'contrary to the national interest', as stated in the government policy. The FIRB will require that construction begin with a specified amount of time. Should a challenge be encountered with construction timing, it is best to be proactive. Go back to the FIRB and explain the situation, and see if an extension can be granted. If you wait and construction does not begin when stated, fines of AU$50,000 for individuals and AU$250,000 for companies can be issued.

Often individuals will choose to migrate to Australia on a Permanent Residence Visa and plan to become Australian citizens at some future date. I caution buyers to proceed with care in attempting to purchase property until their application for the visa is approved. The migration and visa process in Australia is quite complex, and there are no guarantees that you will be approved. If you purchase property prematurely based on the assumption that you will get the visa, and then don't, you may be forced to sell the property and incur a large fine from the FIRB. This could seriously affect your ability to re-lodge your visa application in the future.

Ask for what you want. Ask for help, ask for input, ask for
advice and ideas – but never be afraid to ask.
– Brian Tracy, Business Philosopher

INFORMATION REQUIRED FROM FOREIGN PURCHASERS

THE TYPE OF information that the FIRB will request from you includes your name, address, nationality, type of property you are interested in, as well as a copy of the contract, your passport number, and other details relevant to the type of property you want to purchase. It is important to get good advice from your legal advisor to know all of the requirements for compliance with foreign investment policy in Australia.

THE AUSTRALIAN PROPERTY MARKET

WHEN DETERMINING THE value of purchasing property in Australia, it is helpful to have a good comparison of the market on a global scale. Just as certain areas within a country are better than others, certain countries are more favourable to foreign investors than others. For this reason, if you are considering investing in Australia, it is good to understand the worldwide property trends and what affect each of the markets has on the others.

One of the better sources for this information is a service called Global Property Monitor. They frequently review and update the global property markets, taking into account transaction costs, interest rates, new legislation, and other factors. They also track the movement of the property market in relation to previous months and years, and give forecasts about where they believe the market may be headed. This can be quite useful for foreigners because the property environment in their home countries may be very different from what is currently happening in Australia.

Following are examples of some of the information that can be gleaned from the Global Property Guide. This information compares the first quarter of 2007 with the first quarter of 2008. It is intended as a sample only, and I strongly encourage you to get the latest updated information available prior to investing in property in any country other than your own.

HOUSE PRICE CHANGES AROUND THE WORLD (INFLATION-ADJUSTED)

COUNTRY	YEAR-ON-YEAR		Q-ON-Q
	2007 Q1	2008 Q1	2008 Q1
Bulgaria	17.73	15.21	3.35
China (Shanghai)	-1.28	28.47	1.00
Singapore	13.19	21.56	1.93
Estonia (Tallinn)	-0.44	-6.50	-1.62
Lithuania (Vilnius)	20.65	-7.50	-4.90
Austria	0.79	-2.18	-1.73
Cyprus	8.25	13.26	3.18
South Africa	9.07	-2.55	-2.14
Norway	15.41	-0.28	1.93
Hong Kong (HKU)	1.06	25.93	11.40
Australia (8 Capital Cities)	6.99	9.15	-0.23
Latvia (Riga)	36.53	-38.22	Unavailable
Hong Kong (RVD)	3.28	23.10	6.29
UK (Land Registry)	5.49	0.77	-0.73
South Korea	9.28	-0.83	-0.38
Iceland	0.24	4.78	-2.15
France	4.65	-1.95	-1.73
Japan (6 Major Cities)	7.86	2.89	0.29
New Zealand	10.93	-1.71	0.48
Canada	6.48	4.65	0.51
Finland	3.91	0.05	-1.41

COUNTRY	YEAR-ON-YEAR		Q-ON-Q
Slovakia	13.09	29.30	3.96
Spain	4.69	-0.55	0.42
Indonesia	-0.63	-1.99	-1.63
Greece	3.85	-0.62	0.38
Luxembourg	-0.84	-5.80	-3.17
Netherlands	2.64	0.37	-1.63
Taiwan	0.99	4.71	4.52
Switzerland	2.56	0.91	1.10
UK (Nationwide)	6.00	-1.23	-2.09
Portugal	-0.46	-4.32	-1.37
Israel	-6.89	-3.38	-0.37
Ukraine (Kiev)	63.03	-6.36	-3.84
Japan (National)	-1.38	-1.86	-0.81
Ireland	2.25	-13.24	-3.82
US (Case-Shiller)	-4.05	-18.07	-8.38
US (FHFB)	-4.02	-6.35	-1.57
US (OFHEO)	1.92	-4.16	-2.01

Source: Global Property Guide

AS MANY OF you heard in the media, in 2007 and 2008 the US housing market took a tumble due to a combination of higher interest rates, initially, followed by the tightening credit market and thus the declining property values. The European market has also experienced significant slowdown and a decline in property values. During this time, house prices in the Asia-Pacific region, including Australia, either remained steady or, in some areas, gained momentum.

The best thing about the future is that is only comes
one day at a time.

– Abraham Lincoln (1809 – 65),
President of the United States (1861 – 65)

WHEN YOU LOOK at the preceding chart, it is quite noticeable that some developing countries look as though they made huge gains. However, these countries also experienced large hikes in inflation, so the movement was not as extreme as it may seem. It is prudent to be aware of the monetary climate in any country you consider buying property in, as it could make a tremendous difference in home prices.

ANNUAL HOUSE PRICE CHANGE 2007 (%), ADJUSTED FOR INFLATION

	INFLATION-ADJUSTED	NOMINAL
Singapore	24.29	27.59
China (Shanghai)	20.04	27.85
Bulgaria	15.42	30.59
Estonia (Tallinn)	15.08	23.38
Norway	11.93	11.56
Lithuania	11.43	13.64
Philippines	9.88	13.04
Hong Kong	9.44	11.25
Australia	8.60	10.63
Sweden	7.86	9.86
Japan (6 cities)	7.86	7.75
UK	7.49	9.68
France (Paris)	7.01	8.27
South Korea	6.53	9.01
Colombia	6.40	12.82
Poland	5.81	8.38
New Zealand	4.59	6.67
South Africa	3.77	12.52
Canada	3.66	6.13
Finland	3.29	5.88
Spain	2.88	5.31
Netherlands	2.44	3.77
Denmark	2.29	3.95
Italy	2.08	5.6
Switzerland	1.91	2.56
Malaysia	1.73	3.2
Greece	1.54	4.18
Germany	-0.40	2.04

	INFLATION-ADJUSTED	NOMINAL
Latvia	-1.02	10.22
Indonesia	-1.18	5.24
Japan	-1.38	-1.48
Portugal	-1.68	0.49
Israel	-1.86	-0.51
Thailand	-2.81	-0.78
Ireland	-9.08	-4.68
US (NAR)	-8.46	-5.07
US (FHFB)	-6.79	-3.49
US (OFHEO)	-0.56	1.79

INTEREST RATES ARE a big factor in home prices in every country because the ability to get credit drives the housing market. In Europe, the European Central Bank raised its key interest rate eight times in fifteen months. In the United States, the Federal Reserve Bank raised its key-lending rate seventeen times in twenty-four months between 2004 and 2006. When the property market in the United States turned and started downward, the Fed started lowering its key rate to try and stop the slide. Still, the US housing market continues to weaken. US home prices dropped 5 per cent year-over-year to October 2007, to an average of US$207,800, based on sales recorded by the National Association of Realtors (NAR) (or 8.46 per cent in real terms).

ACCORDING TO GLOBAL PROPERTY MONITOR

PROPERTY PRICES IN Australia continue to recover from the housing market slowdown during 2004 to 2005. The house price index for eight capital cities rose by 10.6 per cent to Sept 2007 from a year earlier, slightly higher than the 10.1 per cent annual increase in Sept 2006. Except for Sydney and Perth, Australia's other major cities all registered house price increases of more than 11 per cent year-over-year to Sept 2007.

The availability of housing finance combined with lack of supply fuelled house price increases in 2007, despite rising interest rates. Population growth from immigration and the skills shortage in the construction sector also contributed to higher prices. Double-digit house price increases are expected to continue in Australia. No drastic changes in immigration policy are expected, now that the Labour Party is in power, and new schemes to assist low income renters and house buyers are likely to increase demand for housing units.

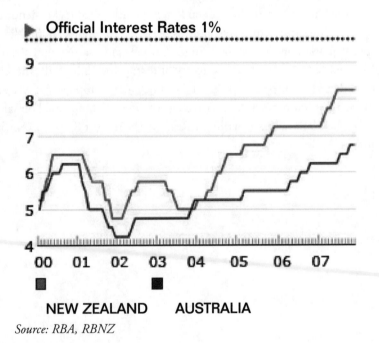

Official Interest Rates 1%

NEW ZEALAND   AUSTRALIA

Source: RBA, RBNZ

216

I do not seek. I find.
– Pablo Picasso (1881 – 1973),
Spanish Artist and Painter

MANY PEOPLE HAVE become involved in property investment over the past several decades, so it's no surprise that they are increasingly buying property outside their own countries. Refer to chapter 10 detailing other countries' property markets.

Investors are looking to duplicate the success they have had in their own backyards by identifying real estate markets around the globe that may offer great opportunities.

Change is the law of life. And those who look only to the past
or present are certain to miss the future.
– John F. Kennedy (1917 – 63),
President of the United States (1961 – 63)

UNFORTUNATELY, FIRST-TIME foreign investors can be surprised by the difference in transaction costs when buying and selling property abroad. In order to gain some insight into the reasons for the variance of these costs, it is necessary to understand the country's legal origin, as most countries with the same origin or basis for their legal system will have a similar process for purchasing property and similar transaction costs.

COUNTRIES GROUPED BY
LEGAL ORIGINS

ENGLISH COMMON LAW: Australia, Canada, Ireland, New Zealand, United Kingdom, United States.

FRENCH COMMERCIAL CODE: France, Belgium, Greece, Italy, Luxembourg, Mexico, Netherlands, Portugal, Spain, and Turkey.

GERMAN COMMERCIAL CODE: Germany, Austria, Japan, South Korea, and Switzerland.

SCANDINAVIAN CIVIL LAW: Denmark, Finland, Iceland, Norway, and Sweden.

SOCIALIST CIVIL LAW: Czech Republic, Hungary, Poland, and Slovakia.

Source: La Porta et al, 1999

COUNTRIES OF FRENCH legal origin, on average, have significantly higher transaction costs (14.2 per cent of the property value) than countries with German (11.9 per cent), Socialist (7.4 per cent), English (6.5 per cent), or Scandinavian (5.2 per cent) legal systems. This is shown in the following chart:

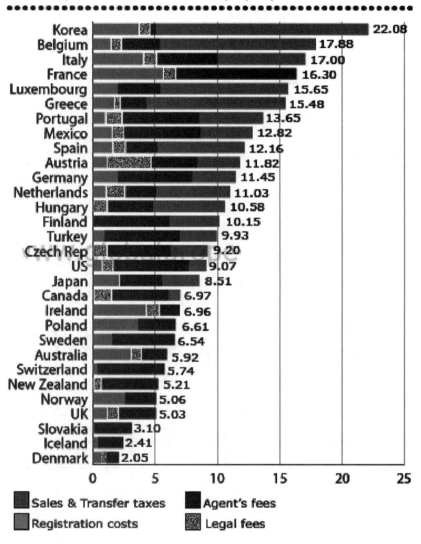

Roundtrip Transaction Cost (% of property value)

Korea	22.08
Belgium	17.88
Italy	17.00
France	16.30
Luxembourg	15.65
Greece	15.48
Portugal	13.65
Mexico	12.82
Spain	12.16
Austria	11.82
Germany	11.45
Netherlands	11.03
Hungary	10.58
Finland	10.15
Turkey	9.93
Czech Rep	9.20
US	9.07
Japan	8.51
Canada	6.97
Ireland	6.96
Poland	6.61
Sweden	6.54
Australia	5.92
Switzerland	5.74
New Zealand	5.21
Norway	5.06
UK	5.03
Slovakia	3.10
Iceland	2.41
Denmark	2.05

Sales & Transfer taxes Agent's fees
Registration costs Legal fees

Source: Global Property Guide

TRANSACTION COSTS ARE considered reasonable if they are near or under 10 per cent, though some countries have costs as low as 3 per cent. You can quickly see from this chart that some countries have excessively high transaction costs – exceeding 20 per cent of the price of the home. This is something to be considered very seriously, as it adds a large amount of cash outlay to property transactions. Even in countries such as Belgium, Italy, France, Luxembourg, and Greece, transaction costs exceed 15 per cent of the property's value. At the other end of the spectrum, the total costs for purchasing a house in Slovakia, Iceland, or Denmark are around 3 per cent or less, and that can make property there quite attractive to the investor. Transaction costs are typically between 5 and 7 per cent in the United Kingdom, Norway, New Zealand, Switzerland, Australia, Sweden, Poland, Ireland, and Canada.

ROUNDTRIP TRANSACTION COST RANGE
(AS A % OF PROPERTY VALUE)

TOTAL COST RANGE			**BUYER RANGE**		**SELLER RANGE**	
COUNTRIES	LOW	HIGH	LOW	HIGH	LOW	HIGH
Australia	3.80	21.15	1.80	9.35	2.00	11.80
Austria	9.40	12.45	7.60	10.35	1.80	2.10
Belgium	13.90	22.10	10.90	18.10	3.00	4.00
Canada	4.68	11.42	1.00	3.00	3.68	8.42
Czech Rep	6.70	9.21	3.70	6.21	3.00	3.00
Denmark	1.31	3.04	0.81	1.04	0.50	2.00
Finland	7.71	10.20	4.05	4.10	3.66	6.10
France	11.06	19.35	8.67	13.37	2.39	5.98
Germany	7.88	12.64	6.09	9.07	1.79	3.57
Greece	11.39	19.01	10.14	16.01	1.25	3.00
Hungary	6.21	13.85	2.61	7.85	3.60	6.00

COUNTRIES	LOW	HIGH	LOW	HIGH	LOW	HIGH
Iceland	1.91	2.52	1.91	2.52	0.00	0.00
Ireland	2.56	15.42	2.56	15.42	0.00	0.00
Italy	10.00	22.10	7.60	18.50	2.40	3.60
Japan	5.76	9.00	6.00	10.00	0.00	0.00
Korea	20.57	21.22	20.57	21.22	0.00	0.00
Luxembourg	11.15	15.65	7.70	12.20	3.45	3.45
Mexico	4.32	17.78	1.28	11.69	3.05	6.09
Netherlands	10.52	13.74	9.33	11.36	1.19	2.38
New Zealand	4.25	5.74	0.21	0.74	4.04	5.00
Norway	3.75	5.70	3.75	5.70	0.00	0.00
Poland	5.55	9.93	5.55	9.93	0.00	0.00
Portugal	5.63	16.05	2.00	10.00	3.63	6.05
Slovakia	2.01	5.50	2.01	5.50	0.00	0.00
Spain	10.66	14.24	8.16	11.24	2.50	3.00
Sweden	4.51	7.50	1.51	2.50	3.00	5.00
Switzerland	3.48	8.93	0.25	3.55	3.23	5.38
Turkey	9.85	10.75	4.60	5.50	5.25	5.25
UK	2.89	14.41	0.54	5.15	235	9.26
US	7.56	11.20	1.05	2.20	6.51	9.00

Source: Global Property Guide research, with input from local real estate agents, government agencies, and the World Bank Doing Business website.

CHAPTER 10
MY AUSTRALIAN PROPERTY

1.   The Foreign Investment Review Board (FIRB) reviews all applications for foreign property investment.

2.   It is important to understand what factors affect the FIRB decision.

3.   Be sure to wait to purchase property if you are applying for a permanent visa in case it is not approved.

4.   Making a property purchase without FIRB approval can result in heavy fines and negatively affect your ability to gain a visa or to immigrate to Australia successfully.

5.   Research the global property market and understand how it may differ from your home country.

6.   It is important that the investor understand the transaction costs of buying and selling property in foreign countries.

7.   Global property forecasts can give the investor great information when evaluating where the best investments may be.

MY ACTION PLAN AND NOTES

_____

_____

_____

_____

_____

_____

_____

_____

_____

_____

_____

_____

CHAPTER
11

MY NEXT STEP:

WHERE TO NOW?

CHAPTER 11

MY NEXT STEP:
WHERE TO NOW?

Carpe diem.
(Seize the day.)
– Horace (65 – 8 BC), Roman Poet

I hear you asking, 'So, where to now?' Well, let's recap on the major points in the book.

As I have made clear, property always has been – and always will be – the best, most simple way for anyone to build wealth, no matter who you are or what your economic condition. Now it's time for you to take the next step and become the property investor of your dreams. It doesn't matter if you've little or no experience. Anyone can be a successful property investor, and I'm proof – if I can do it, anyone can. And if you can learn the few simple techniques outlined in this book, you can make a great income from your property investments.

As I have pointed out numerous times in this text, property millionaires outnumber those of any other investment class, and there's no reason you can't be one of them. Remember, there's nothing wrong with seeing what successful people do and applying those principles to your own life. Property investment is not just for the wealthy. It doesn't really take large sums of money to get involved in real estate. This is because banks will lend up to 90 per cent and sometimes even over 100 per cent against the security of residential property, which means that most people with a steady job and a little capital behind them can afford to buy investment properties.

Another factor contributing to the security of property investment is the high percentage of owner-occupiers, which means people owning or paying off their own homes. Owner-occupiers outweigh investors by a huge percentage, which means that residential property is the only investment market not dominated by investors, and this effectively gives investors a built-in safety net. The rental income you receive from your investment property allows you to borrow and get the benefit of leverage by helping you pay the interest on your mortgage. Over the years, the rental income received from property investments will increase, particularly in times of a slower market.

The ability to use leverage with property significantly increases the amount of profit you can make and, importantly, it allows you to purchase a significantly larger investment than you would normally be able.

Property is a great investment because you make all the decisions, and have direct control over the returns from your property. If your property is not producing good returns, then you can add value through refurbishment, renovations, additional furniture, or other changes that make the property more desirable to tenants. In other words, you can directly influence your returns by taking an interest in your property, and by understanding and then meeting the needs of prospective tenants. You can't do this with other types of investments.

Success does not consist in never making mistakes but in never
making the same one a second time
– George Bernard Shaw (1856 – 1950), Irish Playwright

THERE ARE LITERALLY hundreds of ways you can add value to your property, which will increase your income and your property's capital value and these are only limited by your own imagination. They include items such as giving it a coat of paint, or removing the old carpet and polishing the floorboards underneath. Or you could do major renovations or development works. Unlike most other investments, when property goes up in value, you don't need to sell in order to capitalise on that increased value. You simply go back to your bank or mortgage broker and get your lender to increase your loan. Even if you bought the worst house at the worst possible time, the chances are still good that it will go up in value over the next few years. History has proven that property is possibly the most forgiving investment asset over time. If you are prepared to hold the property over a number of years, it's almost guaranteed to rise in value. There's really no other asset class quite like property!

There's also nothing hard or complicated about investing in property, and there are no secrets that are being kept from you. It is relatively straightforward. You can invest as little or as much as you like. It all depends on how much money you want to make and how determined you are to learn.

You might just choose to buy the odd property here and there, build up a substantial portfolio, or eventually live in a home in the sun. Within a short while, you'll establish a monthly income that just grows and grows – and you hardly have to do anything to get it. This is income or retirement money that you don't have to depend on anyone else to receive. You make it. It's yours and yours alone. Unlike other asset classes, property value never disappears. It won't go bankrupt or drop to zero.

As stated in previous chapters, property investment has several advantages over some other types of investments. This is worth reiterating here to be sure that you understand how important it is.

IT'S INSURABLE

ONE OF THE major advantages of property investing is that it is insurable against most types of loss. This give certainty and confidence to investors to know that they will not lose the value of their investments should something unforseen happen. This is unusual among most types of investments, as they are subjected to a much greater risk of loss. This is one reason that so many wealthy people hold most of their money in real estate. It is subject to much less risk than investments in the open market.

DEPENDABLE AND CONSISTENT CAPITAL GROWTH

CAPITAL APPRECIATION OF residential property in Australia has tracked, on average, at 8 per cent growth per year. This growth is dependable and adds to the investor's wealth each and every year, compounding the value of the property. This means that the value of investment property doubles every seven to ten years. When this appreciation is combined with climbing rental rates over time, the return on the investment is tremendous, and outpaces any other asset class.

YOU CAN USE THE BANK'S MONEY TO BUY

BECAUSE OF THE consistent capital appreciation of property, banks are very willing to loan money on property. This is quite different from other investments where, at most, you might get a percentage of financing for a short period of time. This means that you can use a relatively small amount of your own money and leverage that cash to its maximum advantage, buying multiple properties and financing each one.

YOU CAN INCREASE THE VALUE OF THE INVESTMENT

OFTEN, WHEN ONE invests in shares or other investments, there is no further direct involvement. It doesn't really matter what you do or don't do – the investment is subject to market conditions that you have no control over. This is not true with property. You can take it upon yourself to negotiate a discount when buying, and then add additional value through renovation or refurbishment. This can give you an immediate return on your investment, rather than having to wait for time to pass for it to grow in value. I frequently find properties that can be bought for 20 per cent or more below the current market price, due to a motivated seller. A refurbishment can easily add 10 to 15 per cent to a property. If both of these are combined, then the investor can buy a discounted property, refurbish it, and see an immediate gain in the value of that investment of 30 per cent or better.

GENEROUS TAX DEDUCTIONS AND BENEFITS

THERE ARE NUMEROUS tax deductions and benefits available to the property investor that are not available to those who invest in other areas. Management, every day expenses, maintenance, and many other items are considered deductible expenses. Depreciation and interest expense are also fabulous tools for increased gain through the use of deductions available to the property investor. Any losses from negative cash flow on properties (negative gearing) may also be used to offset other income. It is important to contact a tax accountant who can help you maximise the available deductions and tax offsets.

PROPERTY IS CONSISTENT
AND GIVES YOU CONTROL

YOU HAVE ULTIMATE control over what happens to your property, and how much value you gain from your investment. This means that you make all of the decisions, rather than some executives thousands of miles away whom you don't know and can't influence. You decide what happens to your investment and how much you will eventually gain.

FEAR IS THE ENEMY

I SPENT A great deal of time battling my own fears in relation to investing, and it is unfortunate that many would rather suffer their circumstances than risk making a wrong decision. As I mentioned earlier in this book, I had nearly nothing when I started investing, and I can say I had more than a few fears, but my desire to change my circumstances and my ambition to not be part of the 80 per cent who live on what they earn was stronger than my fear.

To overcome fear, act as if it were impossible to fail,
and it shall be.
– Brian Tracy, Business Philosopher

SOME PEOPLE TOY with the idea of investing in property, merely considering the idea, and then toss it aside out of indifference with the thought that it will take too much effort. How much effort are you willing to put in to secure your future? When you think about the fact that most people get up and go work for at least eight hours every day, not knowing if that job will be there tomorrow, then how can you not justify a bit of time each evening or on the weekend to learn about property investment?

THERE IS NO room for doubt or fear. Everyone started as beginner at one point or another! The advantage you have is that there are so many people who can and want to help you along the way. These are other investors and real estate professionals who can guide and direct you, and don't think they are just in it for a dollar. Property investment can also provide a great source of pride and personal achievement.

WHAT ABOUT THE MONEY?

SO WHAT DO you do if you are strapped for cash and want to get around those high down payments for your investment properties? We talked of numerous solutions, but there is one that is right for you. And if your circumstances change, then there may be a solution that suits you better. Following are just a few:

1. Use the equity in your home. We already touched on this, but it is the easiest and most readily available source of cash for most people. The increased mortgage on your home is even more effective if your home is paid off or nearly so. Every bank has a LVR (loan to value ratio), and this is the maximum they will loan out against a property.

2. I would suggest that if you have a large amount of equity in your home, say in excess of $80,000, you should divide this amount up and look at buying a few properties, using the minimum amount of money down on each one that the bank will accept. I would recommend, if you plan to buy a couple of properties, that you buy the first one and see how you manage for a month or so, and then buy the second property, and so on. I always know all my facts before purchasing a property; for instance, how much the fees, stamp duty, and mortgage repayments will cost, and how much rent the property will achieve. But sometimes it is a great idea to settle into one property at a time, especially if it is your first or second.

3. There is computer software available today that will allow you to enter all your income and expenses and to forecast the growth of the rental

income and property value in coming years. These types of programs are excellent for completing a full presentation of each property you own or buy. The programs will allow you to print report after report so that you can create an impressive document to submit to a lender.

4. Small can be beautiful. Look for lower-priced properties or ones that need some refurbishment. These will generally require a lower deposit, or have owners who are more willing to be flexible on price. You can also look for properties that have the opportunity for an owner live-in/ rental arrangement. One word of caution here is that a lender will be concerned if the property is too small. Most lenders will not lend on a dwelling less than forty square metres in size.

5. Set up your own self-managed superannuation fund, and then use this fund to allow you to purchase rental property – provided it is an outright purchase with no loan or a joint venture with another entity. This means that you either must pay in full for the property or join a group of investors also using Superannuation Funds. Then you can pool your money for outright purchases. This allows money that would otherwise only earn a given rate the chance to earn both cash flow and appreciation. Ask your accountant's advice regarding what a self-managed super fund can and can't do.

6. Consider owner financing. Owner financing, or vendor financing, is much more flexible than anything you might get through a bank or mortgage company, and sellers are many times open to all kinds of creative ideas. So don't be afraid to go this route. It also offers the investor the chance to continue to buy properties, even if they do have a slightly negative cash flow, which can scare off many lenders.

7. Increase your savings. This is not especially thrilling, but it is fine to increase your savings and wait for the right time. Going on a financial diet for a few months is a good idea for most people, whether they are trying to get into property investment or not. Cash gives you so many more options that many people prefer to save up a deposit and then get started, rather than increasing their mortgage – especially if they are first timers.

8. Find partners/family – Sharing the costs of a property with a partner or partners can also be a great way to get into the business, especially if the people you are dealing with are experienced. When two or more people work together, they can afford to take advantage of better financing situations, while spreading the risk equally among them. It is much easier to build a portfolio of properties faster by working together than by working alone. Other partners may also offer you the opportunity to get into different areas of real estate investment that are their particular specialties, such as off-the-plan development opportunities, holiday rentals, or commercial ventures.

THESE ARE JUST a few simple strategies to help you acquire your first property. Once you have accomplished this, you can move on to more advanced financing and leveraging strategies. It is important to know that anyone in any financial situation has options for getting into the real estate investment market. Some options may be easy and some a bit more difficult, but they are there.

ASSEMBLING YOUR TEAM

AS YOU TALK to property investors, you will also want to talk to and find some key professionals to advise you in other areas. Things like taxes, insurance, and legal liability are areas that must be addressed, and getting advice from experts in these fields will save you many dollars down the road. I wish I could say that all advice and help was equal, but it's not, and only by doing your homework can you find those who are really on board with where you want to go.

Experience is one thing you can't get for nothing.
– Oscar Wilde (1854 – 1900),
Irish Dramatist, Novelist, and Poet

IT IS IMPORTANT to find professionals to work with before you start purchasing property. These professionals can help you avoid costly mistakes, as well as understand the tax and legal implications up front.

One of the first professionals you consult should be an accountant who is familiar with property investing. While you may have been told or heard that properties are a great tax deduction, it may or may not be true for you – or at least not as good if you do not receive the right advice. A good accountant will ask for a personal balance sheet, which includes all of your assets and liabilities. He or she will also ask about your income and current obligations. By evaluating your entire income and asset structure, your accountant can tell you what your tax considerations will be, depending on which area of real estate investment you wish to engage in. This reduces the chances of a nasty surprise from the tax office later on, and may influence your decision as to which type of real estate investment you want to engage in, or the financial structure of how you want to purchase property.

One item that is of particular importance in the area of tax deductions is depreciation. It is a great help to obtain a depreciation schedule from an ATO-recognised, qualified expert. Accountants can only calculate the allowable depreciation if they know the purchase price of the item, but are frequently unqualified to calculate the age or installation cost of an item a previous owner installed. This may sound like a small thing, but it can add up to big dollars, as depreciation has a direct effect on your overall investment return, especially if you purchase older properties that have been renovated.

One of the most important professionals you will deal with is a real estate sales agent. These individuals are often the first to hear of new and promising properties that come on the market. It is important to find a sales agent you work well with and can trust. Talk with this person about the type, price range, and the condition of properties you seek. This will keep you from having to hunt for properties by driving all over town, and will allow you to maximise your time attending to other areas of your business. The seller pays sales agents on a commission basis when the deal is finished. They can provide high quality photos of potential properties for investment, and also help you sell properties from your portfolio as the need arises.

Look for an agent who is also an investor, as these agents understand what you are looking for.

SETTING BUSINESS GOALS

MAKE YOUR WISH LIST. You can create the life you want for yourself through property investing. Turn your wishes into goals. Goals are achievable.

Goal setting can be like walking a tightrope. While you don't want to be set your goals so high as to be unattainable, you also don't want to set them too low. Otherwise, you will spend your life underachieving, and even if you reach every low goal you set, you will know that you didn't achieve anywhere near what you were capable of achieving.

In order for a goal to be reached, you must not only create it, but also believe it. Make no mistake – you will have to work for it, sacrifice, and be willing to put in 100 per cent no matter what challenges you face. Remember, winners never quit and quitters never win.

If you want your life to be a magnificent story, then begin by realizing that you are the author and everyday you have the opportunity to write a new page.
– Mark Houlahan

WRITING DOWN YOUR business goals is an important part of the belief process. Though many people set goals once a year, at New Year's or on their birthdays, they often quietly place these goals in a drawer and don't even look at them until the next year. But even they are way ahead of everyone else. A good life takes active planning and participation, and even if you're the once-a-year kind of goal setter, that's better than nothing. But in order to move forward as quickly as possible, it pays to revisit your goals on a weekly and monthly basis. Then, at the end of the year, you can be pleasantly shocked at how far you've come in such a short time, rather than feeling depressed by having the same exact goals for the next year because you didn't accomplish anything.

It is important to be able to articulate what you want from your property investment business it and to write it in such a way as to make it achievable. An effective goal has certain identifiable elements. A good goal is

1. Specifically defined

2. Measurable

3. Attainable

4. Reasonable

5. Time based

MANY OF YOU will recognise this as the SMART model for goal setting that is often used in business. Let's take the first element, specifically defined. You might say to yourself, 'I want to quit my job' or 'I want to retire early'. While these are great ideas, they are not specific, so there's no way to measure how close you are to achieving them – or whether you are falling behind, or ahead of where you should be. A better way to phrase this goal might be, 'I want to make X number of dollars so I can resign from my job at age fifty and retire early'.

Most people respond better to very specific goals than vague goals like, 'do better', or 'be the best'. Specific goals will give you a target to aim for, which will give you some sense of how far you have to go. A good goal will tell you how, when, where, and by what means so that you can track your progress.

FINDING THE RIGHT PROPERTY

THE FOLLOWING QUESTIONS will give answers to the basic guidelines I recommend when seeking the right area and property for you:

1. Do you want capital growth or rental yield?

2. Should you buy in your own area?

3. What type of tenants do you want to attract? What are the demographics of the area?

4. What is happening with the infrastructure, development, and town planning?

5. What types of industry and business support the economy? Is the population growing due to employment?

6. Can you increase the value of the property easily?

7. Where is the area on the property cycle?

8. Where do you find the information you need to evaluate the property?

CAPITAL GROWTH OR RENTAL YIELD

FIRST, YOU MUST decide whether capital growth or rental yield is more important to you. If you decide on capital growth, it usually means that the property will be negative geared, which will create a larger tax deduction each year. If you decide you want to receive higher rental yield or income, it generally means you will see lower growth in the coming years. I am personally a fan of capital growth, as it enables me to leverage into further properties each year with the growth in equity from existing properties. Keep in mind that to continually purchase high-growth properties, you will need good cash flow from other sources of income to help substantiate the mortgage interests while the rental income catches up. I believe that both types of properties have their place in an investor's portfolio, as it diversifies their investments. I would suggest that you speak to your accountant to be sure what is best for your circumstances.

BUYING IN YOUR AREA

THE LOCATION OF a piece of property is one thing that can't be changed, so it is important to get it right. When you are first starting as an investor, I usually recommend that you buy something close to where you live now, or in an area that you know well. Since you may manage some aspects of the property, such as maintenance, there's no use in driving a long distance for a leaky tap. It is also great purchasing your first property in an area that you know well because you will not need to conduct as much research. There will be things you already know about the area, such as what the council has planned, and the main industry and business of the area. Be sure you purchase property based on the numbers and facts and not the emotions you may feel about an area.

Once you have chosen a good area, close to where you live, you will want to look at that area very closely. There are several factors that will determine which particular neighbourhoods should be considered.

Do the homes look well maintained? Are any vacant lots well kept and free of clutter? Nobody wants to live in an area that is in a declining condition, with old cars sitting on the lawn and graffiti everywhere. They want community – a place that looks like home. This is why if you get a good price on a house located in a great area of town that needs a little work, you should seriously consider it, since you know the long-term prospects for this property can be good and you can immediately add value with a renovation.

Look in the immediate vicinity for major employers. The cost of commuting is skyrocketing for most people, so it has become a big factor in considering their housing options. The same is true for retailers. People like to shop close to home, so take note of how close the area is to good shopping areas and restaurants.

Access to things such as major roads, hospitals, utilities, fire stations, and emergency access are also important. Are the roads well maintained? Are there any new construction projects or highways planned that will affect property values? Are the local hospitals, fire stations, and ambulance services readily available and responsive? What utilities are available, and what, if any, new private developments or council projects are planned?

If you invest elsewhere, consider towns with a minimum population of 30,000 to 50,000 people in order to have enough demand for your rental property. This doesn't mean that you absolutely can't invest in a smaller town, but it exposes you to the possibility that your property may stay vacant for longer periods.

NEGOTIATING THE PURCHASE

ONCE YOU FIND the right property, it is time to start your negotiations. Buying and selling property is very much a people business. When a casual observer looks at real estate negotiations, it may seem that there is always a winner and a loser – someone gets the property and someone else gives it up – but that is not necessarily the case. Each party in a real estate deal has a list of wants and a list of needs. As a buyer, the reason for negotiating in real estate is to get all of your needs and most of your wants met. This is also true of the seller.

Buyers can make an offer on a property in which they are interested, and then include what are known as 'subject to' clauses, pending the outcome of due diligence. This accomplishes two things. First, it gives the seller an in-hand offer from a serious buyer so that the seller can confidently take the property off the market. Second, it gives the buyer the ability to accomplish due diligence without fear of losing the property, and also gives the buyer a way out if things are not as they appear to be.

Most contracts in business are simple, upfront transactions. The price is set and agreed upon, and then the paperwork is signed. Both parties are liable to fulfil their portion of the agreed-upon obligations.

Real estate contracts regularly contain specific clauses that allow renegotiation in limited areas. For example, a real estate contract may allow a buyer to get a building and termite inspection report, which they can use to ask the seller to rectify any maintenance issues. Remember, the seller will have the choice to repair the problem, and if they refuse, the buyer has the option to withdraw from the contract. Always protect your interests and add conditions into the contract accordingly. You don't want to be struggling with challenges that could have been prevented, or pay more than a home might actually be worth due to your own short sightedness. While I know contracts and legalese are sleep inducing at times, they are important to your future as a property investor. So don't take short cuts, and make sure you get the best deal possible.

Don't be hesitant to make an offer that is in your best interest. That is what the seller is doing, after all! The whole idea of negotiating is to present your want list to the seller and use that as a starting point.

WHY EMPLOY A PROFESSIONAL PROPERTY MANAGER?

CHALLENGES A LANDLORD can face when managing their own property include

- Legislation

- Tenants who know their rights

- Renting to family and friends

LEGISLATION

TENANCY LEGISLATION VARIES from state to state in Australia. Although the overall principle is similar, the laws are still very different. When I moved from Victoria to Queensland and started investing in real estate in the new area, I had to learn the legislation all over again. It did not really help that I had worked for ten years under Victoria's rental legislation. While the overall concepts were similar, the specific forms, lengths of notices, and types of procedures needed for each situation were all new. For example, one state may allow you to give a tenant notice to vacate the premises if their rent is seven days in arrears. In contrast, another state may require you to issue two breach notices when a tenant is seven days in arrears, and then if they fail to pay their rent, you can issue a notice to leave. If a landlord needs to attend to tribunal hearings, they need to be certain that all their evidence is perfectly complete, as the judge or referee will expect no less.

TENANTS WHO KNOW THEIR RIGHTS

RENTING IS SUCH a common living arrangement today that most people rent a property at some stage of their lives. This being the case, many tenants know their rights, and they are also supplied with full rights and duties booklets when they first move into a property. There are also free advisory boards available to tenants if a tenant receives a notice for vacating, rent increases, entry notices, or for any other reason. They are able to seek advice from these boards, and can receive legal assistance if they choose to dispute a notice.

The purpose of these boards is to help tenants understand their rights and to assist them in understanding the legislation. They also negotiate with the landlords on behalf of the tenants to prevent tribunal attendances. These boards are very helpful, and do prevent situations from expanding into tribunal hearings, which obviously is a better option for all involved.

LANDLORDS RENTING TO FRIENDS AND FAMILY

THIS IS A common situation that results in many families falling out and friendships ending. Many landlords are left to pick up the pieces of relationships after the tenancy arrangements fall apart. Deciding to mix business with family and friends should only be considered and entered into cautiously. Family and friends may take advantage of the landlord due to the mentality that 'the landlord has plenty of money, as the landlord owns an investment property'.

INVESTING IN AUSTRALIA

PROPERTY IS BOOMING in Australia. While other real estate markets around the world have experienced declines, in Australia the outlook remains strong. If you are not an Australian resident and are looking to buy property in Australia, either for investment or to live there, there are several aspects of the real estate buying process that you should understand.

Owner-occupied properties total 70 per cent of the total housing in Australia, which is on par with the United Kingdom. Because Australia operates under a similar common law structure as the United Kingdom, the United States, Canada, Ireland, and New Zealand, the purchase of property is considered rather straightforward and familiar to individuals from those countries. It is very important to note that any foreigner wishing to buy property in Australia must first have the approval of the Foreign Investment Review Board (FIRB).

THE FIRB

THE FOREIGN INVESTMENT Review Board is the advisory board that reviews all necessary applications for foreign property investment against the requirements of government policy. Policies limit certain types of investments by foreigners, while trying to encourage foreign investment in order to help the Australian economy. To this end, there are certain types of properties that are easier for foreigners to buy, such as new construction, as it encourages growth for local areas.

Prior to seeking out properties, it is important to understand the requirements and forms necessary for FIRB approval to be sure that the property you choose conforms to the requirements. You can gain a quick overview of these requirements on the FIRB website at http://www.firb.gov. au. Prospective buyers from certain countries, such as New Zealand and the United States, have been given less strict requirements through legislation. Seeking out a sales agent with experience in dealing with the FIRB can be quite helpful to the foreign investor.

It is better to offer no excuse than a bad one.
– George Washington (1732 – 99),
First President of the United States (1789 – 97)

GET STARTED TODAY!

WHETHER YOU ARE native Australian or a foreigner looking to invest here, the opportunities to create wealth are endless. The biggest mistake you could make right now is to set this book aside and think, 'I'll start buying property soon', and then never do it. This is your opportunity to take control of your financial future and change your life.

I wrote this book with the idea that I could help people who are interested in investing in property but just are not sure where to start. I hope I've made the solution clear and simple. No matter your age or background, anyone can learn the skills necessary to create a fabulous real estate portfolio. The next step for you is to make the decision and go for it. Once you set upon the path to financial freedom, there will be no turning back, and no wondering how you will ever afford to retire. Ten or even twenty years from now, you may look back upon today as the day you decided to change your life. There's nothing stopping you but your own fears. Once those are set aside, the world of success awaits. What are you waiting for? Get started today and don't waste one more minute!

CHAPTER 11
MY NEXT STEP

1.   Property investment has always been one of the best investments.

2.   There is nothing complicated about investing in property – anyone can do it.

3.   Investing in property does not require loads of cash.

4.   Decide what you want and write down your goals.

5.   Get to know professionals who can help you.

6.   Property managers can be a wonderful help as your portfolio grows.

7.   Foreign investors should be aware of the requirements for purchasing property in Australia.

8.   There is nothing standing in your way but your own fears. Get started today and create the life of your dreams.

MY ACTION PLAN AND NOTES

_____

_____

_____

_____

_____

_____

_____

_____

_____

_____

GLOSSARY

GLOSSARY

ACCELERATION CLAUSE

A provision in a mortgage that gives the lender the right to demand payment of the entire principal balance if a monthly payment is missed.

ACCEPTANCE

Consent by the person receiving the offer to be bound by the terms and conditions of the person making the offer. Acceptance of an offer constitutes an agreement. These agreements are enforceable by law.

ACRE

A measurement of land equal to 4047 square metres, or 43,560 square feet.

ACT OF GOD

Any act of nature, such as rain, lightning, floods, or earthquakes. Many insurance policies do not cover losses resulting from an 'Act of God'.

GLOSSARY

ADDITIONAL PRINCIPAL PAYMENT

A payment by a borrower of more than the scheduled principal amount due in order to reduce the remaining balance on the loan.

ADJUSTABLE-RATE MORTGAGE (ARM)

A mortgage that permits the lender to adjust its interest rate periodically on the basis of changes in a specified index.

ADJUSTED BASIS

The original cost of a property, plus the value of any capital expenditures for improvements to the property, minus any depreciation taken.

AGENTS IN CONJUNCTION

You (as a vendor or landlord) may appoint more than one agent, or an appointed agent may act with another agent, who introduces a purchaser or tenant to your property.

ALLOTMENT

A small site for home building, sometimes called a block.

AMENITY

A feature of real property that enhances its attractiveness and increases the occupant's or user's satisfaction with the property, although the feature is not essential to the property's use. Natural amenities include a pleasant or desirable location near water, scenic views of the surrounding area, and so forth. Human-made amenities include swimming pools, tennis courts, community buildings, and other recreational facilities.

ANNUAL MORTGAGOR STATEMENT

A report sent to the mortgagor each year. The report shows how much was paid in taxes and interest during the year, as well as the remaining mortgage loan balance at the end of the year.

ANNUAL PERCENTAGE RATE (APR)

The cost of a mortgage stated as a yearly rate; it includes such items as interest, mortgage insurance, and loan origination fee (points).

APARTMENT

Originally the American word for 'flat', but in Australia it might also be a suite, or just a room that is not necessarily self-contained.

APPLICATION

A form used to apply for a mortgage loan and to record pertinent information concerning a prospective mortgagor and the proposed security.

APPRAISAL

A written or verbal analysis of the estimated value of a property prepared by a qualified appraiser. Contrast with home inspection.

APPRECIATION

An increase in the value of a property due to changes in market conditions (supply and demand) or other causes. The opposite of depreciation.

ARCHITRAVE

A decorative moulding around doors or windows.

ARREARS

Debts, usually rents that have not been paid on time.

ASSESSED VALUE

The valuation placed on property by a public tax assessor for the purpose of taxation.

ASSESSMENT

The process of placing a value on a property for the strict purpose of taxation. It may also refer to a levy against property for a special purpose, such as a sewer assessment.

ASSESSOR

A public official who establishes the value of a property for taxation purposes.

ASSET

Anything of monetary value that is owned by a person. Assets include real property, personal property, and enforceable claims against others (including bank accounts, stocks, mutual funds, managed funds, superannuation, and so on).

ASSIGNMENT

The transfer of a mortgage from one person to another.

AUCTION

A public sale of a property or any real estate that is sold to the highest bidder.

BALANCE SHEET

A financial statement that shows assets, liabilities, and net worth as of a specific date.

BALLOON MORTGAGE

A mortgage that has level monthly payments that will amortise it over a stated term, and which has a lump sum payment due at the end of a specified term.

BALLOON PAYMENT

The final lump sum payment that is made at the maturity date of a balloon mortgage.

BANKRUPTCY

A proceeding in a federal court in which a debtor who owes more than his or her assets can relieve the debts by transferring his or her assets to a trustee.

BEFORE-TAX INCOME

Income before taxes are deducted.

BENEFICIARY

The person designated to receive the income from a trust, estate, or deed of trust.

BEQUEATH

To transfer personal property through a will.

BETTERMENT

An improvement that increases property value, as distinguished from repairs or replacements that simply maintain the value.

BILL OF SALE

A written document that transfers a title to personal property.

BLANKET INSURANCE POLICY

A single policy that covers more than one piece of property (or more than one person).

BLANKET MORTGAGE

The mortgage that is secured by a cooperative project, as opposed to the share loans on individual units within the project.

BODY CORPORATE

An administrative body made up of all the owners within a group of units or apartments in a strata building. The owners elect a committee that handles administration and upkeep of the site.

BONA FIDE

In good faith; without fraud.

BOND

A sum of money paid by a tenant and held by the Rental Bond Board to ensure against defaulting on payment and/or damage to the property.

BOUNDARY

The lines that define the perimeter of a property.

BREACH

A violation of any legal obligation.

BRICK VENEER

A type of construction in which a structural timber frame is tied to a non-load-bearing, single-brick external wall.

BRIDGING LOAN

A short-term loan (usually at a higher rate) taken out to cover the financial gap between buying a new property and selling an existing property.

BROKER

A person who, for a commission or a fee, brings parties together and assists in negotiating contracts between them. See also *mortgage broker.*

BUDGET

A detailed plan of income and expenses expected over a certain period of time. A budget can provide guidelines for managing future investments and expenses.

BUILDING CODE

Local regulations that control design, construction, and materials used in construction. Building codes are based on safety and health standards.

BUSINESS DAY

A standard day for conducting business. Excludes weekends and public holidays.

CALL OPTION

A provision in the mortgage that gives the mortgagee the right to call the mortgage due and payable at the end of a specified period for whatever reason.

CAP

A provision of an adjustable-rate mortgage (ARM) that limits how much the interest rate or mortgage payments may increase or decrease.

CAPITAL

(1) Money used to create income, either as an investment in a business or an income property; (2) The money or property comprising the wealth owned or used by a person or business enterprise; (3) The accumulated wealth of a person or business; (4) The net worth of a business represented by the amount by which its assets exceed its liabilities.

CAPITAL EXPENDITURE

The cost of an improvement made to extend the useful life of a property or to add to its value.

CAPITAL GAIN

The profitable difference between your buying price and selling price. The capital gain is the difference, and is subject to capital gains tax (CGT).

CAPITAL IMPROVEMENT

Any structure or component erected as a permanent improvement to real property that adds to its value and useful life.

CASH FLOW

A measure of cash inflow and outflow from a business. Positive cash flow means more money is coming into the business than is leaving it. Negative cash flow is the converse.

CASH-OUT REFINANCE

A refinance transaction in which the amount of money received from the new loan exceeds the total amount needed to repay the existing first mortgage, closing costs, points, and the amount required to satisfy any outstanding subordinate mortgage liens. In other words, a refinance transaction in which the borrower receives additional cash that can be used for any purpose.

CAVEAT

A warning on a title to a purchaser that a third party might have some interest or right to the property.

CAVEAT EMPTOR

A Latin phrase meaning 'Let the buyer beware'. In other words, the onus is on the buyer to be satisfied with any item before purchasing it.

CBD

Central Business District, the designated business area for a major city.

CERTIFICATE OF DEPOSIT

A document written by a bank or other financial institution that is evidence of a deposit, with the issuer's promise to return the deposit plus earnings at a specified interest rate within a specified time period.

CERTIFICATE OF OCCUPANCY

A document issued by a local government to a developer permitting the structure to be occupied. This generally indicates that the building is in compliance with public health and building codes.

CERTIFICATE OF TITLE

A statement provided by an abstract company, title company, or attorney stating that the current owner legally holds the title to a piece of real estate.

CHATTEL

Another name for personal property; movable items of personal property, such as furniture, that may be included in a sale.

CLEAR TITLE

A title that is free of liens or legal questions as to ownership of the property.

CLIENT

A person who engages an agent or valuer, and who is obliged to pay that agent or valuer a commission or fees.

COLLATERAL

An asset (such as a car or a home) that guarantees the repayment of a loan. The borrower risks losing the asset if the loan is not repaid according to the terms of the loan contract.

COLLECTION

The efforts used to bring a delinquent mortgage current and to file the necessary notices to proceed with foreclosure when necessary.

COMMERCIAL PROPERTY

Premises used for business purposes such as shops, offices, factories, warehouses, and hotels.

COMMISSION

The fee charged by a broker or agent for negotiating a real estate or loan transaction. A commission is generally a percentage of the price of the property or loan.

COMMON AREAS

Those portions of a building, land, and amenities owned (or managed) by a planned unit development (PUD) or condominium project's homeowners' association (or a cooperative project's cooperative corporation) that are used or shared by all of the unit owners, who share in the common expenses of their operation and maintenance. Common areas include swimming pools, tennis courts, and other recreational facilities, as well as common corridors of buildings, parking areas, means of ingress and egress, and so forth.

COMMON LAW

An unwritten body of law based on general custom in England and used to an extent in Australia.

COMPOUND INTEREST

Interest paid on both the original principal balance and on the accrued and unpaid interest.

CONDEMNATION

The determination that a building is not fit for use or is dangerous and must be destroyed; the taking of private property for a public purpose through an exercise of the right of eminent domain.

CONSTRUCTION LOAN

A short-term, interim loan used to finance the cost of construction. The lender makes payments to the builder at periodic intervals as the work progresses.

CONTINGENCY

A condition that must be met before a contract is legally binding. For example, home purchasers often include a contingency that specifies that the contract is not binding until the purchaser obtains a satisfactory home-inspection report from a qualified home inspector.

CONTRACT

An oral or written agreement to do or not to do a certain thing.

CONVERSION MORTGAGE

A special type of mortgage that enables older homeowners to convert the equity they have in their homes into cash, using a variety of payment options to address their specific financial needs. Unlike traditional home equity loans, a borrower does not qualify on the basis of income, but on the value of his or her home. In addition, the loan does not have to be repaid until the borrower no longer occupies the property. Sometimes called a reverse mortgage.

COOLING OFF PERIOD

The legal entitlement of a property purchaser to withdraw from a contract by giving written notice within three clear business days after the Contract of Sale or Contract Note is signed. However, there are some circumstances where the cooling-off period does not apply: (1) when the price of the property, including chattels, exceeds $250,000; (2) when the property is purchased at an auction or within three clear business days of a publicly advertised auction; (3) when the purchaser receives independent legal advice prior to the purchase of the property; (4) if the purchaser is a real estate agent or corporate body; (5) if the purchaser has previously signed a similar contract for the same property; (6) when the property is used mainly for industrial or commercial purposes; (7) or if the property area exceeds twenty hectares and is used mainly for farming. The vendor is entitled to retain $100, or 0.2 per cent of the purchase price, whichever is the greater.

COOPERATIVE (CO-OP)

A type of multiple ownership in which the residents of a multi-unit housing complex own shares in the cooperative corporation that owns the property, giving each resident the right to occupy a specific apartment or unit.

COOPERATIVE CORPORATION

A business trust entity that holds title to a cooperative project and grants occupancy rights to particular apartments or units to shareholders through proprietary leases or similar arrangements.

COVENANT

A clause in a mortgage that obligates or restricts the borrower and that, if violated, can result in foreclosure.

CREDIT

An agreement in which a borrower receives something of value in exchange for a promise to repay the lender at a later date.

CREDIT HISTORY

A record of an individual's open and fully repaid debts. A credit history helps a lender to determine whether a potential borrower has a history of repaying debts in a timely manner.

CREDIT REPORT

A report of an individual's credit history prepared by a credit bureau and used by a lender in determining a loan applicant's creditworthiness.

CREDITOR

A person to whom money is owed.

CUL-DE-SAC

Also called a 'court' or 'dead-end street'. A street with only one entrance, the other end being closed. Often valued for the privacy provided to homes on the street.

DEBT

An amount owed by one person to another. See *instalment loan*.

DEED

The legal document conveying ownership of a property.

DEFAULT

Failure to make mortgage payments on a timely basis or to comply with other requirements of a mortgage.

DELINQUENCY

Failure to make mortgage payments when they are due.

DEPOSIT

A sum of money given to bind the sale of real estate, or a sum of money given to ensure payment or an advance of funds in the processing of a loan.

DEPRECIATION

A decline in the value of property. The opposite of appreciation.

DEVELOPER

A person who buys property and, by improving it (through subdivision, construction, and so forth), increases its value.

DISBURSEMENT

A cash expenditure for the purpose of settling a debt.

DISPOSABLE INCOME

Money left over after all expenses have been met.

DOOR JAMB

The vertical sides and top of a door frame.

DRAWDOWN

The disbursement of loan funds provided by the bank.

DUAL OCCUPANCY

A block of land that is zoned so that two distinct dwellings are permitted to be constructed.

DUPLEX

See *semi-detached*.

EASEMENT

A right of way giving persons other than the owner access to or over a property.

ENCROACHMENT

An improvement that intrudes or overhangs illegally upon another's property.

ENCUMBRANCE

Anything that affects or limits the fee simple title to a property, such as mortgages, leases, easements, or restrictions.

ENDORSER

A person who signs ownership interest over to another party. Contrast with co-maker.

ENVIRONMENTAL IMPACT STUDY

An expert's assessment of the long-term environmental effects of a particular land use/development scheme.

EQUITY

The amount of an asset actually owned; a homeowner's financial interest in a property. Equity is the difference between the fair market value of the property and the amount still owed on its mortgage.

ESTATE

The ownership interest of an individual in real property; the sum total of all the real property and personal property owned by an individual at time of death.

EVICTION

The lawful expulsion of an occupant or tenant from real property.

EXCLUSIVE LISTING

A written contract that gives a licensed real estate agent the exclusive right to sell a property for a specified time, but reserving the owner's right to sell the property alone without the payment of a commission.

EXECUTOR

A person named in a will to administer an estate. The court will appoint an administrator if no executor is named. 'Executrix' is the feminine form.

FAÇADE

The front face of a building.

FAIR MARKET VALUE

The highest price that a buyer (willing but not compelled to buy) would pay, and the lowest a seller (willing but not compelled to sell) would accept.

FAIR TRADING

A government department that determines such matters as business operating to what legislation determines fair business trading.

FEE SIMPLE

The largest possible interest or financial ownership a person can have in real estate.

FEE SIMPLE ESTATE

An unconditional, unlimited estate of inheritance that represents the greatest estate and most extensive interest in land that can be enjoyed. It is of perpetual duration. When the real estate is in a condominium project, the unit owner is the exclusive owner only of the air space within his or her portion of the building (the unit), and is an owner in common with respect to the land and other common portions of the property.

FIBRO CEMENT

Building material made of compressed fibres cemented into rigid sheets.

FINDER'S FEE

A fee or commission paid to a mortgage broker for finding a mortgage loan for a prospective borrower.

FIRM COMMITMENT

A lender's agreement to make a loan to a specific borrower on a specific property.

FIRST MORTGAGE

A mortgage that is the primary lien against a property.

FITTINGS

Objects that can be removed from a property without causing damage to it.

FIXED INSTALMENT

The monthly payment due on a mortgage loan. Fixed instalments includes payment of both principal and interest.

FIXED-RATE MORTGAGE (FRM)

A mortgage in which the interest rate does not change during the entire term of the loan.

FIXTURES

Fixed items that cannot be removed without damaging either the property or the fixture itself, such as cupboards.

FLOOD INSURANCE

Insurance that compensates for physical property damage resulting from flooding. It is required for properties located in federally designated flood areas.

FOOTING

The supports of a building on its foundation.

FORECLOSURE

The legal process by which a borrower in default under a mortgage is deprived of his or her interest in the mortgaged property. This usually involves a forced sale of the property at public auction with the proceeds of the sale being applied to the mortgage debt.

FORFEITURE

The loss of money, property, rights, or privileges due to a breach of legal obligation.

FREEHOLD

An ownership type of real property (real estate) that continues for an indefinite period of time. Freehold estates may be inheritable or non-inheritable. Inheritable estates include the fee simple absolute, the qualified fee, and the fee tail. Non-inheritable estates include various life estates that are created by acts of parties, such as an ordinary life estate, or by operation of law.

GABLE

The triangular part of a building's end wall that extends up to meet the two slopes of a roof.

GAZUMPING

Where a seller agrees to sell to one buyer, but then either sells to another buyer or raises the price when two or more buyers show interest.

GEARING

The ratio of your own money and borrowed funds for investment.

GRANTEE

The person to whom an interest in real property is conveyed.

GRANTOR

The person conveying an interest in real property.

GUARANTEE MORTGAGE

A mortgage that is guaranteed by a third party.

HAZARD INSURANCE

Insurance coverage that compensates for physical damage to a property from fire, wind, vandalism, or other hazards.

HECTARE

The metric measurement of land area equal to 10,000 square metres or 2.47 acres.

HOME INSPECTION

A thorough inspection that evaluates the structural and mechanical condition of a property. A satisfactory home inspection is often included as a contingency by the purchaser. Contrast with appraisal.

HOME UNIT

Individually owned homes in a development of two or more homes; can either be owner occupied, holiday, or permanent rent.

INCOME PROPERTY

Real estate developed or improved to produce income.

INFLATION

An increase in the amount of money or credit available in relation to the amount of goods or services available, which causes an increase in the general price level of goods and services. Over time, inflation reduces the purchasing power of a dollar, making it worth less.

INSTALMENT

The regular, periodic payment that a borrower agrees to make to a lender.

INSTALMENT LOAN

Borrowed money that is repaid in equal payments, known as instalments. A furniture loan is often paid for as an instalment loan.

INSURANCE

A contract that provides compensation for specific losses in exchange for a periodic payment. An individual contract is known as an insurance policy, and the periodic payment is known as an insurance premium.

INSURED MORTGAGE

A mortgage that is protected by the Federal Housing Administration (FHA) or by private mortgage insurance (MI). If the borrower defaults on the loan, the insurer must pay the lender the lesser of the loss incurred or the insured amount.

INTEREST

The fee charged for borrowing money.

INTEREST ACCRUAL RATE

The percentage rate at which interest accrues on the mortgage. In most cases, it is also the rate used to calculate the monthly payments, although it is not used for an adjustable-rate mortgage (ARM) with payment change limitations.

INTEREST RATE

The rate of interest in effect for the monthly payment due.

INVESTMENT PROPERTY

A property that is not occupied by the owner.

IRREVOCABLE

That which cannot be undone.

JOINT TENANCY

A form of co-ownership that gives each tenant equal interest and equal rights in the property, including the right of survivorship.

JOINT VENTURE

Where two or more people or companies combine to carry out a project or enterprise –commonly known as a JV.

JUDGMENT

A decision made by a court of law. In judgments that require the repayment of a debt, the court may place a lien against the debtor's real property as collateral for the judgment's creditor.

JUDGMENT LIEN

A lien on the property of a debtor resulting from the decree of a court.

JUDICIAL FORECLOSURE

A type of foreclosure proceeding used in some states that is handled as a civil lawsuit and conducted entirely under the auspices of a court.

KICKBACK

Payment made to someone for referral of a customer or business. Generally speaking, kickbacks are illegal because, unlike a commission, a kickback is made without the customer's knowledge.

LAMINATED TIMBER

Layers of timber glued and pressed together to increase rigidity or to use as bench tops or cupboard doors.

LAND TAX

A state tax based on the value of a property (not the principal place of residence) that is paid by the owner.

LANDLORD

A person who rents property to another; a lessor; a property owner who surrenders the right to use property for a specific time in exchange for the receipt of rent.

LANDLORD INSURANCE

Insurance that protects a landlord against the loss of rent or rental value due to fire, default of a tenant on their lease, or any other casualty that renders the leased premises unavailable for use.

LATE CHARGE

The penalty a borrower must pay when a payment is made a stated number of days (usually fifteen) after the due date.

LEASE

A written agreement between the property owner and a tenant that stipulates the conditions under which the tenant may possess the real estate for a specified period of time and rental amount.

LEASEHOLD ESTATE

A way of holding title to a property wherein the mortgagor does not actually own the property, but rather has a recorded, long-term lease on it – generally no longer that ninety-nine years.

LEGAL DESCRIPTION

A property description, recognised by law, that is sufficient to locate and identify the property without oral testimony.

LIABILITIES

A person's financial obligations. Liabilities include long-term and short-term debt, as well as any other amounts that are owed to others.

LIEN

A legal claim against a property that must be paid off when the property is sold.

LINE OF CREDIT

An agreement by a commercial bank or other financial institution to extend credit up to a certain amount for a certain time to a specified borrower.

LIQUID ASSET

A cash asset or an asset that is easily converted into cash.

LOAN

A sum of borrowed money (principal) that is generally repaid with interest.

LOAN-TO-VALUE RATIO (LTV) PERCENTAGE

The relationship between the principal balance of the mortgage and the appraised value – or sale price if it is lower – of a property. For example, a $100,000 home with an $80,000 mortgage has a LTV percentage of 80 per cent.

MANAGING AGENT

A licensed real estate agent authorised by you to manage your property.

MANHOLE

An opening that permits access to the space between the roof and the ceiling, or below the floor.

MARGIN

For an adjustable-rate mortgage (ARM), the amount that is added to the index to establish the interest rate on each adjustment date, subject to any limitations on the interest rate change.

MARKET PRICE

The actually price paid for a property (market value is only an estimate).

MATURITY

The date on which the principal balance of a loan, bond, or other financial instrument becomes due and payable.

MEZZANINE

An intermediary floor, usually between the ground and first floors.

MEZZANINE FINANCE

A high-yielding investment in property development, filling the gap between bank lending and the developers' own equity, sometimes with a second mortgage over the property.

MODIFICATION

The act of changing any aspect of a property.

MONTHLY FIXED INSTALMENT

That portion of the total monthly payment that is applied toward principal and interest. When a mortgage negatively amortises, the monthly fixed instalment does not include any amount for principal reduction.

MONTHLY PAYMENT MORTGAGE

A mortgage that requires payments to reduce the debt once a month.

MORTGAGE

A legal document that pledges a property to the lender as security for payment of a debt.

MORTGAGE BROKER

An individual or company that brings borrowers and lenders together for the purpose of loan origination. Mortgage brokers typically require a fee or a commission for their services.

MORTGAGE INSURANCE

Mortgage insurance that is provided by a private mortgage insurance company to protect lenders against loss if a borrower defaults. Most lenders generally require MI for a loan with a loan-to-value ratio (LVR) percentage in excess of 80 per cent.

MORTGAGE INSURANCE PREMIUM (MIP)

The amount paid by a mortgagor for mortgage insurance, either to a government agency such as the Federal Housing Administration (FHA) or to a private mortgage insurance (MI) company.

MORTGAGEE

The lender in a mortgage agreement.

MORTGAGOR

The borrower in a mortgage agreement.

MULTI-DWELLING UNITS

Properties that provide separate housing units for more than one family, although they secure only a single mortgage.

MULTIPLE DWELLING

A building with more than three units/apartment.

NET CASH FLOW

The income that remains for an investment property after the monthly operating income is reduced by the monthly housing expense, which includes principal, interest, taxes, and insurance for the mortgage, homeowners' association dues, leasehold payments, and subordinate financing payments.

NET WORTH

The value of all of a person's assets, including cash, minus all liabilities.

NO CASH-OUT REFINANCE

A refinance transaction in which the new mortgage amount is limited to the sum of the remaining balance of the existing first mortgage, closing costs (including prepaid items), points, the amount required to satisfy any mortgage liens that are more than one year old (if the borrower chooses to satisfy them), and other funds for the borrower's use (as long as the amount does not exceed 1 per cent of the principal amount of the new mortgage).

NON-LIQUID ASSET

An asset that cannot easily be converted into cash.

NOTE

A legal document that obligates a borrower to repay a mortgage loan at a stated interest rate during a specified period of time.

NOTICE OF DEFAULT

A formal written notice to a borrower that a default has occurred and that legal action may be taken.

NULL AND VOID

That which cannot be legally enforced, as with a contract provision that is not in conformance with the law.

OFF THE PLAN

To purchase a property before it is completed, after having only seen the plans.

OMBUDSMAN

A department that helps the consumer if any wrongdoing has occurred. The Australian Banking Industry Ombudsman (ABIO) is the avenue through which a customer can make a complaint about their bank and have it dealt with independently.

OPEN LISTING

A type of listing agreement in which more than one real estate agent may be employed to sell the property. The owner pays a commission only to the agent who finds the buyer. This listing is also known as a simple listing or a general listing, and the owner is not obligated to pay anyone a commission if the owner personally sells the property. Builders and developers, who agree to pay a sales commission to any agent who sells a house or lot in their subdivision, often use such a listing.

OWNER FINANCING

A property purchasing transaction in which the property seller provides all or part of the financing.

PASSED IN

The term for when a property fails to reach the buyer's reserve price at auction. (The highest bidder has the right to meet the reserve price, or to try to negotiate an acceptable price.)

PAYEE

One who receives a payment.

PAYOR

One who makes a payment.

POWER OF ATTORNEY

A legal document that authorises another person to act on one's behalf. A power of attorney can grant complete authority, or can be limited to certain acts and/or certain periods of time.

PREPAYMENT

Any amount paid to reduce the principal balance of a loan before the due date. Payment in full on a mortgage that may result from the sale of the property, the owner's decision to pay off the loan in full, or a foreclosure. In each case, prepayment means payment occurs before the loan has been fully amortised.

PRE-QUALIFICATION

The process of determining how much money a prospective homebuyer will be eligible to borrow before he or she applies for a loan.

PRIME RATE

The interest rate that banks charge to their preferred customers. Changes in the prime rate influence changes in other rates, including mortgage interest rates.

PRINCIPAL

The amount borrowed or remaining unpaid. The part of the monthly payment that reduces the remaining balance of a mortgage.

PRINCIPAL BALANCE

The outstanding balance of principal on a mortgage. The principal balance does not include interest or any other charges. See *remaining balance.*

PROPERTY SYNDICATE

A group that is formed, under a legal agreement/structure, to invest in a property asset for a specific term.

PUBLIC AUCTION

A meeting in an announced public location to sell property to repay a mortgage that is in default.

PUBLIC LIABILITY

The insurance taken by one's self to protect one's self against claims made by members of the public who might be injured in some way on the property.

PURCHASE AND SALE AGREEMENT

A written contract signed by the buyer and seller stating the terms and conditions under which a property will be sold.

QUANTITY SURVEYOR

A professional who calculates the materials required for the construction, and also helps you to compile the depreciation schedule for taxation purposes.

RAFTER

Part of the framework of the roof, rafters slope down from the ridge to the eaves.

GLOSSARY

REAL ESTATE AGENT

A person licensed to negotiate and transact the sale of real estate on behalf of the property owner.

REAL PROPERTY

Land and appurtenances, including anything of a permanent nature, such as structures, trees, minerals, and the interest, benefits, and inherent rights thereof.

REDRAW FACILITY

A loan where the borrower can make additional payments and then access those funds when required. There may be a minimum redraw amount.

REFINANCE TRANSACTION

The process of paying off one loan with the proceeds from a new loan, using the same property as security.

REI

The Real Estate Institute of Australia is a national representative body of real estate agents. REIV is the representative body in Victoria, REIQ in Queensland, and so forth.

REMAINING BALANCE

The amount of principal that has not yet been repaid.

REMAINING TERM

The original amortization term minus the number of payments that have been applied.

REPAYMENT PLAN

An arrangement made to repay delinquent instalments or advances. Lenders' formal repayment plans are called 'relief provisions'.

RESERVE PRICE

The lowest price that a seller will accept at auction.

REZONING

A planning term in which the local authority can alter a planning code to allow a change in use. Can also be called 'change of use'.

RIGHT OF FIRST REFUSAL

A provision in an agreement that requires the owner of a property to give another party the first opportunity to purchase or lease the property before he or she offers it for sale or lease to others.

RIGHT OF WAY

A right of one property or the general public for access to or across another property.

ROOF PITCH

The slope of a roof.

SASH

The frame in which a pane of glass is set to form a window.

SECOND MORTGAGE

A mortgage that has a lien position subordinate to the first mortgage.

SECURED LOAN

A loan that is backed by collateral.

SECURITY

Property that is pledged as collateral for a loan.

SELLER'S MARKET

When demand for property is greater than supply, it results in greater opportunities for owners, who may find someone willing to offer the asking price or even a figure greater than the asking price. Contrast with *buyer's market*.

SEMI-DETACHED

Also called duplex; a type of construction where two buildings are attached together by a common wall.

SERVICING

The collection of mortgage payments from borrowers, and the related responsibilities of a loan servicer.

SETTLEMENT

(1) The sale of a property is finalised by the legal representatives of the vendor and the purchaser, mortgage documents come into effect, costs are paid, and the new owner takes possession of the property; (2) The sinking of the soil or any part of the structure which it supports.

SILL

The horizontal section of material at the base of a window opening.

SKILLION

A roof shape consisting of a single sloping surface without a ridge.

SPECIAL CONDITION

A condition that must be met before a contract is legally binding. For example, if buying a home, the purchaser may specify that the contract is not legally binding until the purchaser has obtained a building inspection.

SPECULATOR

A person who buys a property with the expectation of selling it later for a higher price.

SQUARE

A square is a measurement of home area. One square = 9.3 m² approximately.

Home Area- Squares to Square Metres											
Squares 7	8	9	10	10	11	11.5	12	12.5	13	13.5	14
m²	65	75	85	95	100	100	105	110	115	120	125	130
Squares 14.5	15	16	17	18	19	20	22	24	26	28	30
m²	135	140	150	160	165	175	185	205	225	240	260	280

STAMP DUTY

A state tax on conveyance or transfer of real property calculated based on the total value of the property (including chattels). This calculation varies from state to state.

STANDARD PAYMENT CALCULATION

The method used to determine the monthly payment required to repay the remaining balance of a mortgage in substantially equal instalments over the remaining term of the mortgage at the current interest rate.

STRATA TITLE

A title to a unit or lot on the plan for a subdivision associated with townhouses, units, and blocks of flats, and based on the horizontal and vertical subdivision of air space. Owners have a certificate of title, are absolute owners of a freehold flat, and have an undivided share of the common property.

SUBDIVISION

A housing development that is created by dividing a tract of land into individual lots for sale or lease.

SURVEY

A drawing or map showing the precise legal boundaries of a property, the location of improvements, easements, rights of way, encroachments, and other physical features.

TENANCY IN COMMON

A type of joint tenancy within a property without the right of survivorship. Contrast with tenancy by the entirety and with joint tenancy.

THIRD-PARTY ORIGINATION

A process by which a lender uses another party to completely or partially originate, process, underwrite, close, fund, or package the mortgages it plans to deliver to the secondary mortgage market. See *mortgage broker.*

TITLE

A legal document evidencing a person's right to or ownership of a property.

TITLE SEARCH

A check of the title records to ensure that the seller is the legal owner of the property and that there are no liens or other claims outstanding.

TORRENS TITLE

Named after Sir Robert Torrens of South Australia, it is a system of recording property ownership where registration on the Certificate of Title guarantees ownership. This system is now used in many parts of the world.

TOWNHOUSE

A dwelling unit, generally having two or more floors and attached to other similar units, via party walls.

TRANSFER OF OWNERSHIP

Any means by which the ownership of a property changes hands. Lenders consider all of the following situations to be transfers of ownership: the purchase of a property 'subject to' the mortgage, the assumption of the mortgage debt by the property purchaser, and any exchange of possession of the property under a land sales contract or any other land trust device.

TRUSTEE

A fiduciary that holds or controls property for the benefit of another.

UNDERPINNING

Supports placed under an existing wall to provide added strength.

UNDERWRITING

The process of evaluating a loan application to determine the risk involved for the lender. Underwriting involves an analysis of the borrower's creditworthiness and the quality of the property itself.

GLOSSARY

UNIMPROVED CAPITAL VALUE

The value of a piece of unencumbered land without any improvements.

UNREGISTERED MORTGAGE

A mortgage that is not registered on the title to a property.

UNSECURED LOAN

A loan that is not backed by collateral.

UTILITIES

The private or public service facilities, such as gas, electricity, telephone, water, and sewer, which are provided as part of the development of the land.

VENDOR

Seller.

VENDOR TERMS

When a property is paid for over a period of time.

VESTED

Having the right to use a portion of a fund, such as an individual retirement fund. For example, individuals who are 100 per cent vested can withdraw all of the funds that are set aside for them in a retirement fund. However, taxes may be due on any funds that are actually withdrawn.

VILLA

A single storey attached dwelling.

WALL CAVITY

The space between the inner and outer sections of a wall.

WATER COURSE

A natural stream of running water being fed by a natural source, such as a stream or river.

WITHOUT PREJUDICE

These words used during a negotiation mean that any suggestion or plan put forward cannot be used as evidence later if the negotiations break down.

YIELD

The interest earned or return received by an investor on an investment, stated as a percentage of the amount invested.

ZONING

Local authority guidelines for the permitted use of land.